CAN I TOUCH YOU JESUS?

CAN I TOUCH YOU JESUS?

A Journey of Faith and Divine Encounters

DESIREE DANTAS

© Purelilly Press

Contents

Dedication

To my beloved family, whose unwavering support and love have been my guiding light on this writer's journey inspired by God's command. To Bruno and Dayan, your love and respect have been my strength, propelling me forward with each word penned. This book is dedicated to you, my pillars of support and source of endless inspiration.

In memory of Geny, my mother, and Dalmy, my father.

Endorsements

What a blessing it will be for you to read through this anointed book Desiree has written, "Can I Touch You Jesus?"

This book offers profound insights into the boundless and transformative love of God, tailored specifically for you. Through a collection of personal testimonies, it delves into the author's journey of reaching out to the Lord and experiencing His presence on a daily basis, even having the privilege to touch Him. As you read, you'll discover how to encounter His presence and receive the same intimate experience.

Desiree passionately conveys God's desire for each individual to know His love deeply and to walk with Him through every circumstance. While reading through its pages, I could feel the powerful presence of the Holy Spirit surging through my being, reassuring me of His presence and touch. I'm confident you'll also encounter the sweet presence of the Lord.

I highly recommend this captivating book—it's truly hard to put down. Consider sharing copies with your family and friends as a blessing. As you delve into its pages, you'll come to realize that touching Jesus is within reach for all.

Lorene Keling
President, NASA Aglow Lighthouse, Webster, Texas

When Desiree asked me to read and write a short forward for her book "Can I Touch You Jesus," I was so honored. This book is a wealth of stories and revelation of how precious you are to Jesus and the healing He brings to your soul when you let him touch your life. I pray this book touches your life as it did mine.

Robyn Thom Rodgers

When Moses was on the mountain with God, in Exodus 33:17-23, Moses said, "Show me your glory." Moses had grace in the sight of God and God showed Moses His glory. God's glory is too awesome for any person to see though, so God covered Moses with His hand while God's face passed by.

Like Moses, Desiree Dantas asked Jesus to show himself to her and He did. As our intercessor and bridge to God, Jesus is able to show God's glory to us in a way that we can handle. Jesus manifested himself to Desiree and even allowed her to touch Him. Yes, she touched the one and only Son of God and Son of Man, the King of Kings, and Lord of Lords. Immediately, her life was changed and her perspectives on life became eternal. In her book, Can I Touch You Jesus? Desiree shares her experience with Jesus and the eternal perspectives that have been imparted to her since her encounter.

Stuart Rich
Teacher of Bible Studies at Praise Chapel, Webster, Texas

I

Encountering Jesus: A Transformative Moment

In my journey with God, I often felt as though I had broken wings, leading me to seek spiritual healing independently and explore various religions. Reflecting now, I understand that while some paths I ventured on were misguided, they also held the potential to lead me astray. I've come to recognize that seeking religion alone isn't the ultimate solution; rather, it's the pursuit of a relationship with God that truly matters. Discussions around religion are often contentious with believers in Christ on one side and nonbelievers on the other. Now I know that for me, it's more about cultivating a genuine relationship with God rather than by adhering to a strict set of rules. I liken this relationship to the intimacy and closeness one shares with devoted friends. As a believer, I once struggled with the misconception that had to be perfect to earn God's love, fearing a distant and judgmental God. However, at my bedside on my twenty-third birthday, I had a profound in-person encounter with Jesus. This experience totally redefined my understanding of God's love for me, and I knew finally the depth of God's concern for me.

Reflecting back on my childhood now, I realize that I dismissed many supernatural experiences as mere coincidences, failing to recognize them as God's attempts to draw me closer to Him. God was giving me signs that He wanted to be closer to me. I believed this kind of intimacy with God was only for special people. My encounter shattered the notion that such experiences were reserved for special individuals. I was just a simple girl in search of God. Now, I understand that God's love is unconditional, even for imperfect believers like me. I share this experience to encourage others who may be struggling with guilt and shame. Let me emphasize that a personal connection with Jesus requires nothing more than our belief, acceptance of His grace, following His teachings, and asking His forgiveness. It is not based on how perfect you are, and the depth of your connection does not depend on how many supernatural experiences you experience first-hand. You, like me, might take for granted what is happening in the supernatural concerning you, and you may not realize all the things God is doing on your behalf to protect you and let you know He is seeking to have a connection with you.

Matthew 7:7 underscores that God eagerly awaits our seeking and knocking for a relationship with Him. We only need to ask God into our lives, and He will not disappoint us.

Ask, and it shall be given you; seek, and ye shall find; knock, and it shall be opened unto you. (Matthew 7:7 KJV)

The memory of encountering the image and power of Jesus on that significant night of my twenty-third birthday remains deeply ingrained, though it took time to fully grasp and articulate the encounter to others. I encourage you to pursue your own personal encounter with God, for He eagerly awaits your seeking heart. Describing such an experience is akin to attempting to convey the exquisite taste of ice cream without having tasted it firsthand. God stands ready to unveil His boundless love to you, and I wholeheartedly believe that He cherishes the simplicity of acts of kindness amidst the self centeredness prevalent in our world.

My Birthday Gift

On the night of April 4th, my twenty-third birthday, at AM, Jesus appeared to me in the form of a human-shaped light. Here's what happened:

The night before, I prayed to Jesus with a simple request 'Jesus, I know you speak to me, but tomorrow is my birthday and I hope to receive your presence as a birthday gift. If it's not too much to ask, I know you are real! Could you come and show yourself to me?'

I had always felt upset on my birthdays, as the enemy would lie to me, saying I was not worthy to be born. Because of this, I would often feel depressed and wouldn't want to celebrate. After my prayer asking Jesus to show up, I drifted off to sleep.

My bedroom was small, with my low bed positioned beside a large wooden window. That night, I woke up in the early hours, startled by a bright light shining in my face, and I saw a figure of a man in the form of light standing there. At first, I didn't want to believe it; I thought it might be one of my siblings playing a trick by turning on the lights. I asked, "Could you turn the lights off?"

The light spoke back to me, saying, "You asked me to come. I'm here!" Initially, I thought I was dreaming and told myself, 'I'm dreaming.' But the voice responded, "No, you're not dreaming; you're awake. You asked me to come, and I'm here.

I asked, "Who are you?"

"I'm Jesus," He said.

I continued to doubt, repeating to myself, 'I'm dreaming, I'm dreaming...' Once again, Jesus spoke to me, saying, "No, you're not! You're awake, and you asked me to come. I'm here. Look around. You're in your room, on your bed." I looked around, seeing my window and examining the details of my room. I even touched my arms to confirm that I was indeed awake. How did I know it was truly Jesus? I just knew it was Him. Despite my doubts and uncertainties, this was truly happening! His telepathic thoughts and His presence provided evidence. He appeared as a form of light, radiant and bright!

I asked Him if I could touch Him. I knew that if He was who He said He was, I would feel something incredibly special upon touching Him, assuring me of His real presence. There are many mocking spirits out there, so we must be careful, for the angel of darkness often masquerades as an angel of light to mislead godly people. So, I asked, "Can I touch you?"

"Sure!" He replied.

And so, I touched Him—Jesus, the Son of God, the 'I AM'! My body felt His holy fire, and this sensation lasted until morning. When I woke up, my siblings were walking into my room with candles to celebrate my birthday. I was upset with them, asking why they would come into my room and shine lights in my face, pretending to be Jesus. They looked at me as if I was crazy, not understanding my question. At that moment, an inner voice spoke to me, saying, 'This was Me! Never doubt my presence again! For now, don't speak with anyone about it. Keep it to yourself until I tell you otherwise!' And in my mind, I responded, 'Yes, Jesus!' He has continued to speak to me many more times.

A Spiritual Awakening

My encounter with Jesus left an indelible mark which transformed me. Describing the experience of being in His divine presence is challenging, as words inadequately convey the profound emotions that engulfed me.

In every situation, God's hands are at work. The promise, "I will never leave you nor forsake you," resonates with the truth. His tangible presence orchestrates events according to His divine will. He is always with you no matter what you do or where you are.

The writing of this book was guided by God's discreet hints, urging me to carefully discern the messages hidden within. It emphasizes the importance of a second look, urging a deeper understanding of God's wisdom and the meanings that only He himself unveils.

Jesus consistently implores me to share this encounter, knowing that belief and doubt may intermingle among those who hear it. Whether people believe me or not, I know that it is He, Jesus, who encourages the sharing of this story and the stories that came after. He has assured me they are like spiritual seeds. I am confident none of those seeds will be lost.

This profound truth was highlighted to me by the Holy Spirit in the most inconsequential moment; through the act of discarding an orange seed into the trash! The act served as a reminder that God teaches us through everyday events.

Wrap-Up: Through encountering Jesus and experiencing a spiritual awakening, God initiates a transformative journey in our lives, inviting us to embrace His presence and truth.

Reflective Questions:

My encounter with Jesus and my search for the truth of God transformed my perspective on life and faith. Reflect on your search for the truth and encounters you have had with God. Can you think of everyday moments when you knew God had his hand on your life?

If you have never taken the time to simply ask God to make himself known to you, stop and ask him now. I know that he will show you a sign. In what ways have you experienced a spiritual awakening in your relationship with God?

2

Divine Connections

When Jesus visited me, it was an amazing experience! I had been searching for truth for some time, so I prayed for a visit from the Lord Himself. It was hard to wrap my mind around the encounter! I initially thought I was being visited by an angel, or having a really vivid dream. While I believe in heavenly angels, I have no doubt I was being visited by our savior Himself in person. For when I asked, "Who are you?" the Lord said, "I am Jesus!" He came himself! He did not send an angel. But why did Jesus Himself come; you might ask? I can tell you that I had been praying fervently up until that point, and I specifically asked for Him to come to me in person. This made me realize that God likes us to be specific. He wants us to be clear and specific when dealing with Him. In other words, God is into the details. The Bible says we have authority; therefore, we know that authority is something God wants us to learn about— the power to command over things, animals, situations with people, and even angels. It's a level of power over diseases, demons, and everything that moves. We have the God-given authority and the ability to make decisions, direct outcomes, and influence circumstances.

Spiritual Beings

In the Bible, angels often show up when people face trouble. Take Daniel, for example. In the story of Daniel in the lion den, Daniel, a trusted servant in the Babylonian court, faced opposition from jealous officials. They tricked King Darius into signing a decree forbidding prayers to any god or man except himself, for thirty days. Knowing about the decree but remaining faithful to his God, Daniel continued to pray to his God in spite of what he might face.

Caught in the act, Daniel was thrown into a den of lions as punishment. Miraculously, God sent an angel to shut the lions' mouths, and Daniel emerged unharmed the next morning. Witnessing this, King Darius praised Daniel's God and acknowledged the God of Israel as the living God. When Daniel was in the lion's den, the Lord sent an Angel to protect him and keep him alive! It's funny to think that when we're in trouble, the chances of being protected by an angel are greater. So, being in trouble might not be so bad after all! It could be a chance to see God move on your behalf. We must ask ourselves, what exactly triggers such strong protection from angels or from God Himself? Is there a formula? Is it a strong request, a powerful prayer, or simply having a faithful heart?

We know the bible says that God made our spirits before creating everything else. In Genesis 1:26, it says, *"Let us make mankind in our image, in our likeness."* This means we're designed to rule! We are designed to rule over animals and everything that moves on the Earth.

We are a mix of our body - our outer person, our spirit - our inner most person, and our soul - our mind where our emotions come from. We are a triune being - spirit, soul, and body - all created by God. This physical body governs the physical world around us and has authority over the animals and everything that moves. So, who are angels and why are they here?

Angels are spirits. Those under God's authority are commanded by God to help humans do God's work. They act like colleagues, bringing joy to all mankind. They are here to bring God's messages, protect, interfere, break bondages, and fight against God's enemies.

Fallen Angels

The book of Genesis tells us that not all angels are good. There were angels that disobeyed and left God. They are not here to protect. They are "self-centered angels," also known as the fallen angels.

Jude 1:6 mentions these fallen angels who abandoned their proper dwelling and are bound in darkness for judgment on the great day.

And the angels who did not keep their proper domain but left their own abode, He has reserved in everlasting chains under darkness for the judgment of the great day. (Jude 1:6 NKJV)

Visited in My Dreams

Jesus or His Angels often come in my dreams, helping me make decisions. Often, these dreams need to be interpreted, and I pray and meditate on them. I always start with asking God to help me understand what He was showing me in the dream.

One dream stands out in my memory, and it involves everyone reading this book. The dream started with the sky opening up with a circle of God's angels. Several people in the dream became scared, but Christians prayed, and I marveled at the power of God. In my spirit I knew this dream was about things to come. In the dream, I was explaining to my husband that it was the day of Rapture, where God's people would be saved from evil and protected, and I saw evil shrinking down in fear of God's formidable power!

God has used dreams in my life since I was a small child. As I've had many dreams, I believe God wants me to use them in my own life and to advise others about His kingdom. God desires a connection with us every day through supernatural experiences.

I know that God has given his angels charge over me because even as a small two-year-old child, I recall falling downstairs in a two-story duplex and coming out of it without a scratch. I genuinely believe I was caught by an angel that day. God gave me recall of this incident, and I realize now that a spiritual being was holding and protecting me as I fell. I know I had God's favor and protection even then. Who knows how many times we have been through something that could have been so much worse had it not been for God's divine intervention. Two scriptures stand out to me.

The angel of the LORD encamps all around those who fear Him, and delivers them. (Psalm 34:7 NKJV)

For He shall give His angels charge over you, to keep you in all your ways. (Psalm 91:11 NKJV)

Always remember, God has a plan for you!

As we go about our daily routines, Jesus wants to use us. In our busy lives, finding time to read the Bible and meditate on it can be challenging and sometimes feel impossible to fit in. I asked Jesus why we are so busy, and He answered, "I didn't create man to be busy like this. I created man to have joy, do my works, and have time for a relationship with me!"

When I began thinking about authoring this book, it wasn't just my idea. Jesus told me to write it, to let people know. Though I didn't see myself as a writer, He assured me He would give me instructions on what to write. So, I followed His guidance.

Each one of us has natural God-given talents to serve God in various ways. You, too, can ask God to use you every day. Despite the fear of writing a book about my experiences, I decided to trust Him with it. I did it even though fear came over me. We can be sure that God always sends help either by an angel or by the Holy Spirit to guide us in His given mission. In this case, to author a book about all the revelations He has given me. Sometimes you can't see it, but that doesn't mean God and his angels are not there. Always obey God. When it's God's mission, I know He'll be with you!

Write it Down!

One notable thing I remember is that God asked me to "write it down." Your visions and ideas should be put on paper, turning them into reality. I've had this habit since my teenage years — write it down so you won't forget, then read it over and over to stay focused. If it's a prayer, it will be heard.

There is a scripture that confirms what the Lord showed me about writing down the vision.

Then the Lord answered me and said:

"Write the vision and make it plain on tablets, that he may run who reads it. For the vision is yet for an appointed time; but at the end it will speak, and it will not lie. Though it tarries, wait for it; because it will surely come, it will not tarry." (Habakkuk 2:2-3 NKJV)

Although there are many Bible scriptures that talk about angels and describing their roles in obeying God's will, I will leave you with these two.

Then I raised my eyes and looked, and there were two women, coming with the wind in their wings; for they had wings like the wings of a stork, and they lifted up the basket between earth and heaven. (Zechariah 5:9 NKJV)

But to which of the angels has He ever said: "Sit at My right hand, till I make Your enemies Your footstool"? Are they not all ministering spirits sent forth to minister for those who will inherit salvation? (Hebrews 1:13-14 NKJV)

Angels are there to minister and serve us — how cool is that! When you are obedient in God's assignment for your life, His angels help you to see it come to pass!

Signs

Some people are seers, able to see the spiritual realm as Jesus reveals it to them. There's no limit to what they can see — vast open revelations of the future, miracles, or revelations on how they can serve Jesus. They too are used for God's kingdom purpose. God has many ways of revealing himself to people, not just angels.

So, it does not matter If you've never seen or felt an angel or seen Jesus. Please don't get upset. Know, truly, that God loves His people and will find a way to reach them for His purpose. Just like how Jesus revealed Himself to the apostles after the resurrection. Jesus might come in person and even allow physical touch like He did with doubting Thomas. Thomas was one of Jesus' disciples. He said he would have to touch Jesus' hands and put his hand on Jesus' side where he was pierced by a spear on the cross, to believe Jesus' was resurrected and was alive.

The Holy Spirit can manifest in dreams, as light, o through a small whispering voice. God uses angels and othe signs, like animals, objects, numbers, or people who are i tune with Him and reach out. My son, for instance, alway sees the number 33 everywhere. For him it reminds him tha Jesus is in the midst. Jesus was 33 years old when He wa crucified, and I believe that Jesus wants my son to know H died for him. God cares about you specifically. He is all abou the details of your life and knows how to reach you. It is u to you to make time for Him and give Him your undivide attention and seek Him out.

Wrap-Up: Through divine connections and the indwellin presence of Jesus, God takes the initiative to deepen our spir itual bond with Him, leading us into a closer relationship.

Reflective Questions:

Reflect on a time when you felt a divine connection or sensed th presence of Jesus in your life. How did it impact you?

How does knowing that Jesus dwells within you change your ap proach to daily life and relationships?

3

Divine Presence Within

When you really want to follow God and believe in Him, it opens up a way for Him to talk to you. It might already be happening, but finding a quiet moment in your heart is important. It's tough to hear Jesus' voice when life feels like a hurricane and the storm is tossing you around, and you can't catch a break. But when Jesus is around, He changes the atmosphere and things change. His voice comes through even in the middle of life's biggest storms because He really loves you and wants to talk to you, bless you, and be there for you, just like He was there for me that night at my bedside.

On that night, something incredible happened. God decided to show up for me. What I saw on that night was a pure light, bright, and shining so strong I could barely look at it for more than a few moments. Believe me, I tried! I asked him if He was Jesus three times. I still could not wrap my mind around the moment, and I said to myself, 'I'm dreaming. I don't think this is real.' He told me to look around, to look at my room. Then He said to look at my body, lying down on my bed. I looked around, and yes it was! Still grappling with my unbelief at this phenomenal moment. I said, "If you are Jesus then can I touch you?" He said, "You are not dreaming, and yes, you can touch me!" So, I reached out, and I touched Him the wonderful great Jesus! His power went passing through my body, and His light filled me with His peace. Again, it was a magnificent encounter with my Lord and Savior, Jesus!

The Bible says that God is no respecter of persons.

Then Peter opened his mouth and said: "In truth I perceive that God shows no partiality. But in every nation whoever fears Him and works righteousness is accepted by Him.' (Acts 10:34-35 NKJV)

This passage emphasizes that God's acceptance and favor are not based on a person's nationality, race, or social status. Instead, those who fear God and live righteously are accepted by Him, regardless of their background.

I know in my heart that God will show up for anyone who loves Him deeply. But remember, He is still God. You can't force God to show up. All you can do is ask, trust and wait. Jesus doesn't follow our schedules; He has His own perfect timing. He shows up with Heaven's light, brightening the darkest parts of our soul, setting us free from bondage and leading us to truth, proving that He's real in amazing ways.

I've seen people who've had experiences with Jesus or angels. I believe that in special moments, either Jesus, the Holy Spirit, or His angels will show up to minister to you.

For He will command his angels concerning you to guard you in all your ways; they will lift you up in their hands, so that you will not strike your foot against a stone. (Psalm 91:11-12 NIV)

I think everyone has at the very least, two angels with them for their whole life. I am still in awe I got to touch Jesus. It was a special moment. He came personally to talk to me, proving who He was and building my faith. We have such a loving God!

Now, when Jesus spoke to me, He was saying, "Here I am, the 'I AM,' I am Jesus!" It changed everything for me. My communication with Jesus reached a new level.

On many occasions, whether I am facing challenges, or He is revealing His plans for me, I now clearly recognize and hear His voice. For example, today while getting ready for work, I heard a simple word, "sentry." I knew God was sharing something with me, so I looked it up, and it means a soldier stationed to keep guard or to control access to a place. Jesus is our watchman or sentry. He keeps guard over our spirit and His angels watch over and protect us. Markedly, the word sentry was not familiar to me because English is not my first language. My first language is Portuguese. Jesus told me the word sentry in my native language so I couldn't miss its meaning over my life and yours.

Jesus is All Things

When Jesus says, "I am," He means I am your salvation, I am your healer, I am your internal peace, and I am your financial source whatever you need at the moment. He is saying I am your source for everything in your life.

The Lord created the Earth for you, and all the stars you see in the skies are there for us to admire so that you might worship Him. A reminder for when you go to sleep that He is there with you until you wake up. At the moment you were born, God was pleased with you as His creation, and the world around you is a gift from the Lord Himself. Everything good thing you have is from Him. Nothing comes to you without His knowledge. When you get in sync with God, i.e. you are on the same page, circumstances will change for the good. God wants you to know that when you worship Him it is like a beautiful fragrance of a flower in the air, and when you praise Him with your thoughts and words, it shines to Him like the most beautiful of galaxies. God is worthy of our praise!

Entering In

Many Christians walk by faith, but the true gift and promise of faith is entering the realm of the Holy Spirit, a deeper faith where angels and true power reside. Psalms 91 calls it the secret place.

> He who dwells in the secret place of the Most High
> Shall abide under the shadow of the Almighty.
> I will say of the Lord, "He is my refuge and my fortress;
> My God, in Him I will trust."
> Surely He shall deliver you from the snare of the fowler
> And from the perilous pestilence.

He shall cover you with His feathers,
And under His wings you shall take refuge;
His truth shall be your shield and buckler.
You shall not be afraid of the terror by night,
Nor of the arrow that flies by day,
Nor of the pestilence that walks in darkness,
Nor of the destruction that lays waste at noonday.
A thousand may fall at your side,
And ten thousand at your right hand;
But it shall not come near you.
Only with your eyes shall you look,
And see the reward of the wicked.
Because you have made the Lord, who is my refuge,
Even the Most High, your dwelling place,
No evil shall befall you,
Nor shall any plague come near your dwelling;
For He shall give His angels charge over you,
To keep you in all your ways.
In their hands they shall bear you up,
Lest you dash your foot against a stone.
You shall tread upon the lion and the cobra,
The young lion and the serpent you shall trample underfoot.
"Because he has set his love upon Me,
therefore I will deliver him;
I will set him on high, because he has known My name.
He shall call upon Me, and I will answer him;
I will be with him in trouble;
I will deliver him and honor him.
With long life I will satisfy him,
And show him My salvation." (Psalm 91 NKJV)

How do we manifest all this in our lives? It is by having true faith, believing above our expectations, and expecting miracles. Jesus is there waiting for us to seek Him; observing and perfecting the work He has already done in us.

God patiently waits for those who don't believe in Him, continually rescuing them in His special ways, in His perfect timing. If we dive deeper into His love, and exhibit true repentance, limitless miracles will happen.

Don't Limit God

We often limit the Lord, but He is the unlimited God of the universe! Have you ever looked into a telescope? We can't count the stars, but God knows each one and has named them, just like He knows each one of us. Before we were formed in our mother's womb, He knew our names. Looking at the stars, I see God's creation in the dimension of His eyes that's never-ending, infinite, and filled with amazing grace!

> *Have you not known?*
> *Have you not heard?*
> *The everlasting God, the Lord,*
> *The Creator of the ends of the earth,*
> *Neither faints nor is weary.*
> *His understanding is unsearchable.* (Isaiah 40:28 NKJV)

God is so creative; He's the mastermind of everything. He is El Shaddai, the incredible God of all creation.

Genesis 35:11 says, "I am God Almighty..." He who said to the world, "Enough," creating the limits between the Earth and the heavens. He made the atmosphere breathable. He didn't just create us, He breathed life into us. He provided a comfortable environment for us to exist in. This beautiful place, He created for us.

The more I think about God's creation, the more amazed I become. From the smallest, invisible creatures to dinosaurs, not as history books tell us, but uniquely detailed creations. God loves details, and when He imagines things, they form with shapes, colors, and complete uniqueness. I once watched a Christian television show, and the guest speaker shared that she had an encounter with God. When she looked into Jesus' eyes, she saw Him forming her in her mother's womb. Jesus is so amazing! He wants us to see where we came from—we are from the pupil of His eyes.

For by Him all things were created that are in heaven and that are on earth, visible and invisible, whether thrones or dominions or principalities or powers. All things were created through Him and for Him. And He is before all things, and in Him all things consist. (Colossians 1:16-17 NKJV)

Truly Blessed

I'm blessed with wonderful people in my life. Through tough times, my parents prayed for me. God has also put good people in my life to be like parents, offering support in every battle. This was crucial for me. Because often, as young people, we might not think anyone cares about us, and assume our parents, or the people that are supposed to care for us, understand what it is we're going through. If you feel this way, let me assure you that God sees everything we do, not with eyes of condemnation, but with eyes of love. God is the perfect parent.

One day my son came home, and I wanted to make his favorite food and talk to him with love about his life. I desired so much to connect with my son. It is the same with God. I will never forget when the Lord spoke to me and said, "It's the same for Me with you. I want to give you everything, be with you all the time, love you unconditionally, and care for you, just like you do for your sons." The feeling after He spoke stayed in my heart for many days, revealing the unconditional love God has for me, like the love of my father and mother combined.

God loves you unconditionally and His desire is to have a personal relationship with you.

For I am persuaded that neither death nor life, nor angels nor principalities nor powers, nor things present nor things to come, nor height nor depth, nor any other created thing, shall be able to separate us from the love of God which is in Christ Jesus our Lord. (Romans 8:38-39 NKJV)

Wrap-Up: We've journeyed through profound encounters with God, explored the depths of faith and witnessed the boundless love of God. We've emphasized the importance of trust, patience and faith in experiencing God's presence and miracles. We've discovered God's greatness and power and His great desire to have a close relationship with you.

Reflective Questions:

How has your understanding of divine presence and communication with God changed through the experiences shared in this chapter, and what steps will you take to deepen your relationship with God?

In thinking on Desiree's encounter with Jesus, which profoundly impacted her faith have you even had a similar experience or felt the presence of God in your life? If so, how did it shape your beliefs and actions moving forward?

4

We Are Covered By His Blood

Let me tell you a touching story about a grandpa who wanted his grandson to grasp the profound love of Jesus. The grandson was going through a rough patch with drugs, and the family tried everything to help him. One day, the grandpa did something quite extraordinary. He held a gun to his own face, saying, "This is what Jesus did for you!" Now, he wasn't trying to harm himself, but rather to illustrate the depth of Jesus' sacrifice. The family hoped this vivid act would make the grandson realize the seriousness of his situation. The grandpa wanted him to have a visual representation that Christ willingly took on the cross and shed his blood on the boy's behalf. And praise God, it worked! The grandson turned his life over to Christ and quit drugs. This not only saved his soul but affected his whole family. Of course, this is simplified version, this story goes beyond a simple tale; it's about discovering freedom and genuine happiness through accepting the love of Jesus.

This world is not an easy place. It is full of lies and deceptions. There is not one of us who has not experienced it. I've experienced it too. In life, chasing temporary joys may briefly satisfy, but they won't fill the void within us. Only the pure love of Jesus can complete us. I've personally felt His intense love, a feeling that lingers even now. Trusting in His promises, I face challenges — be it sickness, failed deals, or personal mistakes — with praise and patience. Waiting isn't just an act; it's a practice of patience and faith, elevating us to a higher spiritual realm in accordance with God's timing.

Broken Pieces

One day when I was cleaning my closet, I found a plethora of old jewelry with missing parts and broken pieces. I forgot I even had the box. I had saved it in case I needed to repair my jewelry. I separated it and began to look at what I could make with it. So, I started to glue parts together, and soon I began to transform this junk jewelry into new beautiful bracelets! In the middle of cutting this and fixing that, God began to speak to me.

"See these old pieces? At one time, it was all perfect, but after being used many times, it broke and began to look ugly. Then you came and fixed them and put them together. Now, they are better than before!" He continued, "See now, I do the same thing for humanity. I made man perfect, but life brought disappointments, confusion, wrong beliefs. It all fell apart. But now, when you call me, I am there waiting for you to mend the broken pieces of your heart. I can make everything new. I can put the broken pieces together and make beautiful again!"

When we are separated from God, we are like broken jewelry that needs to be repaired by the hands of the Almighty. He is the master jeweler who puts "The Rock, Jesus" in the center to shine again as an original piece. Wow! When I looked at the bracelets after I finished, I was so pleased that God used my broken jewelry pieces to explain to me how He works on us, making us new!

Wrap-Up: By covering us with His blood and restoring us from brokenness, God initiates a process of redemption and renewal, offering us grace and wholeness.

Reflective Questions:

In what ways has God's grace covered you in times of brokenness or sin?

How has God used brokenness in your life as a catalyst for restoration and spiritual growth?

5

Healing Inside Out: The healing of the Soul

T he phrase "by His stripes we are healed" is from the Bible, specifically, Isaiah chapter 53 and I Peter chapter 2.

But He was wounded for our transgressions, He was bruised for our iniquities; the chastisement for our peace was upon Him, and by His stripes, we are healed.

(Isaiah 53:5 NKJV)

...who Himself bore our sins in His own body on the tree, that we, having died to sins, might live for righteousness – by whose stripes you were healed.

(I Peter 2:24 NKJV)

You may have heard these scriptures before and the phrase, "by His stripes, we are healed," many times in church sermons and on church TV and wondered what it meant. It's a powerful message about Jesus' sacrifice on the cross for all of us, not just a select few. Even the worst of us, the ones who seem undeserving (like that neighbor you might not like) -- the scripture holds true for them as well. Even for that drug dealer who sold drugs to a kid. Jesus died for the best of us, and the worst of us. He died for all men and women. We are all God's creation, flawed and prone to sin until we pass away. Some of us have really messed up, and we do not know our true identity in Christ. God's grace toward us and his choice to be sacrificed for us, forever transforms us through God's ability through Jesus to forgive the unforgivable. We are cleansed through our repentance and belief in the sacrifice Jesus made. The whipping He took before he was crucified cut Him severely, causing the stripes on his body. Those are the stripes that healed you. He bore sickness and disease in His body so we don't have to. We are not only forgiven for our sins but promised our healing inwardly and outwardly; forever changed.

Personally, I have seen God work in my own life. Once, I was dealing with back pain, and instead of just asking God for healing, I re-read the healing verses of the Bible in order to align my mind with what God says belongs to me. Each day, the pain lessened. The word of God emphasizes that Jesus desires to heal our bodies as well as our souls. Diseases often manifest when we distance ourselves from God's words, getting entangled in distractions that consume more of our time than God does. God is well aware of how the way we think and believe affects our body and mind. What we believe or have faith in can either bring death or life to us. In fact, the Bible says to renew your mind every day to what the word of God says. When we find ourselves caught up more in worldly matters or entangled in sin, we open doors for the enemy and the kingdom of darkness to bind us up physically and mentally, creating a spiritual bondage in our minds and souls. This allows a curse to take hold in our life. To break free from bondage and curses that come with it, it's absolutely essential to read the word of God, meditate on the promises of God concerning you as a believer, and reorient yourself toward kingdom minded thinking. You too can be healed, in and out, by simply pressing in and believing that what the word of God has to say about you is for you and is your inheritance. Here are a few scriptures to meditate on today.

Bless the Lord, O my soul, and forget not all His benefits: who forgives all your iniquities, who heals all your diseases. (Psalm 103:2-3 NKJV)

If you diligently heed the voice of the Lord your God and do what is right in His sight, give ear to His commandments and keep all His statutes, I will put none of the diseases on you which I have brought on the Egyptians. For I am the Lord who heals you. (Exodus 15:26 NKJV)

Wrap-Up: Through healing the soul from within and leading us on a journey to spiritual wealth, God initiates a process of inner transformation and abundance.

Reflective Questions:

Reflect on a time when God brought healing to your soul or provided spiritual wealth in your life. What did you learn from that experience?

How can you continue to pursue inner healing and spiritual growth in your relationship with God?

6

Social Media Bondage

We have all lost hours scrolling through social media, flipping through screen after screen with most of them ending one message, pointing us in one direction. What is that direction you ask? We are constantly bombarded with notions of what anyone other than our creator says means to be happy" and dictate the paths we should follow for this fulfillment. If you take a moment and really focus on the messages, it only takes a minute to see that society says to be happy, we need to lose weight, buy a car, buy stuff, get a better house, get more money, get the latest course, follow the latest fad. The list of expediential things that are supposed to make you happy go on and on. No matter how you get it, by winning the lottery, working hard, finding the latest get rich quick scheme, it is easy to get trapped in the "need vacuum" thinking we need the latest and greatest no matter what it is. The truth is, everything costs something and takes time and hard work. Someone has to pay for it, someway, somehow. find it is wisdom to realize that time is a precious commodit that God has given us to fulfill his purpose in life. So, whe I am overwhelmed with that little voice in my head sayin that I need the latest purse or I need to read every email c check my iPad or check my messages, I stop and ask mysel 'All these things seem urgent, but are they important? Ar they part of God's success plan for me?' I realize God know better than I do what it is I truly need in my life, and wher I need to be spending my time. The Bible says that God has plan laid out for us, and His plan is perfect. It is important t understand true happiness comes from fulfilling the purpos God placed in you. The enemy wants to steal that from you.

For example, writing this book was a challenge for me. knew God had instructed me to write things down, but I di not feel much inspiration. I began to realize that social medi was consuming of my attention. I was not pressing into th things God had for me to write down. Breaking the bondag meant giving God my undivided attention and asking Hin to help me overcome distractions that were keeping me fron focusing on the lessons He had for me to share. Well, you se the outcome, the bond is broken because you are seeing th book is written. Praise God! You can ask God to help yo focus, to give you wisdom, and to overcome the pull of th world which seeks to pull you in so many different direction away from God. Please know that with God's transformativ power and physical and mental healing, we can align ou desires with His purpose. True happiness comes from fulfill ing God's true purpose.

Wrap-up: Social media can make us feel like we need to chase after things that the world says will make us happy, like buying stuff or following trends. It can distract us from God's real plan and purpose for our lives. Desiree learned that true happiness comes from following God's plan for our lives. In pursuing God's plan and focusing on His word and a true relationship with Him, she was able to break free from the hold social media had on her.

Reflection Questions:

How have daily distractions like social media affected what you think will make you happy? Have you ever felt pressured to chase after things that the world says are important, rather than what God says is important for you?

Desiree talks about the importance of asking God for help to stay focused on what really matters. How do you make sure you're paying attention to God's plan for your life, especially when there are so many distractions around?

The chapter highlights the transformative power of God's influence through His word and the Holy Spirit in helping us to redeem our thoughts and shape our world. How will you prioritize your daily time with God?

7

In the Middle of the Storm

Sleep eluded me as I tossed and turned waiting for God's response to a very special prayer. My mind was racing, and I contemplated the issues I needed to resolve. Watching the clock, time seemed to slow down. Instead of continuing to battle for sleep, I decided to get up. I resigned myself to sit down with a cup of instant soup and start writing down what I thought the Lord wanted me to write down.

The months prior had thrown numerous challenges my way. Starting with shutting down my business, relocating, and more...much more. Initially I was perplexed and paralyzed by the simultaneous upheavals. While some want a crystal ball when life starts unfolding challenges, I have learned to take one step at a time and face each step by asking God, "What's next?" His directives prompted changes in various aspects of my life. Little did I know, a huge unwanted challenge and surprise was headed my way. Although I was trying to go down the paths God was directing me to take, there was no doubt I was struggling and battling sin. My husband and I both were dabbling in sin, and our marital relationship was in real jeopardy. Although I did not know it, God had been working on my husband who was also struggling, and he decided to go to church without my trying to coerce him. Remarkably, my husband, who had been distant from God, was now experiencing God's love and mercy amid all of our relationship struggles. In the midst of my and my husband's own shortcomings, God intervened, urging us to change. One day, Jesus appeared to him, instructing a course correction, and my husband entrusted God with this new journey. I remember him calling me that day, voice trembling, "Honey, come get me. I can't drive. God spoke to me!" From that moment, transformation commenced. Our relationship improved, but there was another surprise the Lord had been preparing me for. My husband received the diagnosis of stage 4 colon cancer. Unfortunately, this was familiar territory for me. I had been here before with my grandfather and with my father. The diagnosis was a huge wake up call for both of us. His doctors said he needed surgery to remove the cancer. Despite the dreadfulness, this diagnosis is what changed our lives, our marriage, and our focus on God. During this season a church prophet foretold an encounter with God, and during surgery, it happened. During surgery, God spoke to my husband and instructed him to change. God's message to him was prompting a removal of sin from his life. The day after, my husband conveyed God's message: "SIN NO MORE!" Thus began our

ourney through cancer recovery, anchored in the belief that
e are all healed through Jesus' sacrifice. Despite all we were
acing we decided to believe God is capable of anything. And
he words that we lived by from that moment on were these.

> *Fear not, for I am with you.*
> *Be not dismayed, for I am your God.*
> *I will strengthen you,*
> *Yes, I will help you,*
> *I will uphold you with My righteous right hand.*
> (Isaiah 41:10 NKJV)

I decided to put this verse on our refrigerator. I commit-
ed to read it every day and proclaim it over my life. Now I
now that just because things aren't unfolding as you think
hey should does not mean God is not working behind the
cenes on your behalf.

Vrap-up: Amidst the noise of the world and adversity, God
akes the initiative to guide us and offer true happiness,
nviting us to find peace and contentment in Him.

Reflective Questions:

How do you seek God's guidance and find true happiness in the midst of life's challenges and distractions?

Reflect on a time when you experienced God's peace and guidance during a difficult situation. What did you learn about His faithfulness?

8

Dreams

When God wants to communicate with me, He often chooses dreams as a distinct way to convey important messages. He emphasizes the significance of paying attention, differentiating these dreams from common ones, as they serve as a unique channel to reveal His favor over me and those connected to my life. As I've mentioned, our communication is a two-way street—I talk to God, and He responds. It's a heavenly relationship where He speaks to me by allowing me to see, hear, feel, or have dreams.

I've observed a recurring theme in my heavenly dreams—an image of a lion. About two weeks before the Passover of 2020, I had a vivid dream. While walking, I noticed a lion on my right side. Our eyes met, and I hurriedly ran towards a door, locking myself inside to protect against the lion. Outside, I saw other people, and the lion was biting someone on the shoulder. The dream felt exceptionally real, and God spoke to me, saying, "Stay at home. Put blood on the doors and protect yourself and your family until this ends."

Putting "blood on the doors" is a reference to the Passover. God did not want me to literally put lamb's blood on my doors. He meant it metaphorically, to speak God's protection over my home and family and have faith in Him during this difficult time. Let's review the Passover from the book of Exodus.

During the time when the Israelites were enslaved by Egypt, God sent Moses back to Egypt to tell Pharaoh to let His people go so they may worship Him. Because Pharaoh disobeyed and would not let them go, God had no choice but to judge their wrongdoing. Egypt had enslaved and mistreated the Israelites for many, many years. Ten plagues struck Egypt. The last plague caused the death of all the first-born Egyptian males. God told the Israelites, through Moses, to sacrifice a lamb and place its blood on the doorposts of their dwellings. When the judgment was enacted, God "passed over" the Israelite homes. Some people say God was evil and unjust to allow this judgement. However, it is because they do not know that Pharoah had ordered the murder of Hebrew boys at birth. For God to be good, He must be just. That horrific sin could not go unpunished. The sin Pharoah enacted upon the Israelites came back upon himself and the Egyptians as judgement. Here is the account of Pharoah's order from the book of Exodus.

Then a new king, to whom Joseph meant nothing, came to power in Egypt. "Look," he said to his people, "the Israelites have become far too numerous for us. Come, we must deal shrewdly with them or they will become even more numerous and, if war breaks out, will join our enemies, fight against us and leave the country."

So they put slave masters over them to oppress them with forced labor, and they built Pithom and Rameses as store cities for Pharaoh. But the more they were oppressed, the more they multiplied and spread; so the Egyptians came to dread the Israelites and worked them ruthlessly. They made their lives bitter with harsh labor in brick and mortar and with all kinds of work in the fields; in all their harsh labor the Egyptians worked them ruthlessly.

The king of Egypt said to the Hebrew midwives, whose names were Shiphrah and Puah, "When you are helping the Hebrew women during childbirth on the delivery stool, if you see that the baby is a boy, kill him; but if it is a girl, let her live." The midwives, however, feared God and did not do what the king of Egypt had told them to do; they let the boys live. Then the king of Egypt summoned the midwives and asked them, "Why have you done this? Why have you let the boys live?"

The midwives answered Pharaoh, "Hebrew women are not like Egyptian women; they are vigorous and give birth before the midwives arrive."

So God was kind to the midwives and the people increased and became even more numerous. And because the midwives feared God, he gave them families of their own.

Then Pharaoh gave this order to all his people: "Every Hebrew boy that is born you must throw into the Nile, but let every girl live." (Exodus 1:8-22 NIV)

The ten plagues were a series of divine interventions aimed at liberating God's people from the hands of Pharaoh and judging Egypt for their sins. It's a powerful reminder of God's protection and the importance of obeying Him.

Every step of the way through each plague God protected His people and gave them instructions to follow. When they obeyed, they were kept from harm. In case you do not remember, or have only seen it in movies, here are the ten plagues of Egypt. You can read the account in Exodus, chapters 7-12.

1. Water to Blood
2. Frogs
3. Gnats
4. Flies
5. Pestilence of Livestock
6. Boils
7. Hail
8. Locusts
9. Darkness for Three Days
10. Death of Firstborn

Pharaoh finally orders the Israelites to leave, taking whatever they want, and even asks Moses to bless him in the name of the Lord.

After having my lion dream, I found myself compelled to act. Following a divine nudge, we took communion at home, using grape juice as a symbolic representation of Jesus' lood. I even applied small amounts of grape juice on our oors, an act of faith for God's protection. I have a profound onviction that adhering to God's word and following his ommandments will act as a shield for our home, family, and ommunity.

I have navigated through the challenges of coming to a ew country. I have encountered hurricanes and floods, experiences that had never happened to me before and were bsent in my homeland. The community's resilience and support during such times left a lasting impression on me. I was n awe of how people reached out and supported one another. Now, fast forward to the global pandemic—COVID-19—a ituation reminiscent of the plagues in Egypt. With government advising and urging people to stay indoors, I felt the Lord's prompting to replicate the Passover action by using he grape juice symbolically, applying the blood of the lamb Jesus) over our doors. This act, although symbolic, resonated with my deep belief in God's power to ward off harm to my amily. This was an act of faith and obedience.

Acknowledging the inevitability of contagious diseases, I ind solace in Jesus's sacrifice and his promise of healing because of the cross. The Bible says that repentance is a pivotal tep, signifying our trust in Jesus for healing and a return o our original spiritual identity aligned with God's word. The ongoing pandemic is viewed as a clarion call, prompting amilies to come together, fostering unity, and shifting our dependence from human efforts to unwavering faith in God. This period of hardship serves as a training ground, instilling esilience and elevating our faith as we learn to live not by ear, but by faith.

Knowing God in the Last Days

We have often heard the last days referred to the Rapture. The story of the rapture talks about God's people being spared from the trouble of this world and pulled out at the last minute. This begs the question, who will be left behind?

The Bible in 1 Thessalonians says that Jesus will return for his church. Are you ready?

> For the Lord himself will come down from heaven, with a loud command, with the voice of the archangel and with the trumpet call of God, and the dead in Christ will rise first. After that, we who are still alive and are left will be caught up together with them in the clouds to meet the Lord in the air. And so, we will be with the Lord forever. (1 Thessalonians 4:16–17 NIV)

More movies are coming out about the last days and the return of Jesus Christ for his church. Have you ever watched movies depicting the Rapture? It's said that in an instant, in a moment, true believers will vanish before your eyes, to join Christ. This will be God's way of pulling them out of the trouble and saving them from the worst kind of evil in this world. Much like Noah being told to build an Ark and prepare, we are told to prepare now. The ones left behind will no doubt be in a massive state of confusion and fear. There will even be well-known religious leaders who are shocked because they are also left behind. There's a common misconception that being religious is the answer and will safeguard you from being left behind, but in truth, it is our hearts that

God wants. We need to be sold out and walking in peace with Jesus.

More and more we keep hearing, even from non-Christians, that we are living in the last days, but the Bible says that no one knows the exact instant Jesus will return. We don't know when He will call us home either by rapture or by our death, but we can be sure that each one of us has our appointed time on this earth. The choice between spiritual life and death is given to us, and the choice is critical. There are two types of death; one is spiritual and one is physical. Spiritual death is more severe than physical death; it's a life without meaning here on earth or thereafter.

The essence of life goes beyond material possessions. No matter how much we accumulate on earth, we can only take our souls in the rapture or when we pass away. In contemplating the rapture-themed movies, there's a poignant element—the bewilderment of those left behind. I believe it will be true that in that time there will be great speculation about what happened to the ones that are gone. Many people will have never heard of the scripture you just read. They will not know the words of the Bible about Christ Jesus coming back for us, nor will they have the knowledge of the salvation that Christ died and rose again so that we might have eternal life. Or, more sadly, they will have chosen to ignore it.

If only all people would embrace the truth and accept Jesus as their Lord and savior and pray with a sincere heart the prayer asking for salvation, asking for forgiveness of sins, and acknowledging Christ as Lord of their life. If they only understood how easily accessible God is, and how He wants to show them the path to Heaven, I believe they would act, receive the gift of salvation, and actively encourage others to join in. It's a simple yet profound act. We only need to look around to see the truth that we are, according to scripture, approaching the end, and there's a palpable spiritual sense in the air. Natural events are intensifying, and historical plagues are resurfacing. While some might argue that such occurrences have always been part of the world, God reveals the deeper truth—except for Jesus, it may get worse before getting better.

Examining Biblical passages, we find the apostles faced their worst nightmares and deaths to be with Jesus. In one incident, the disciples, who were devoted believers, were in the midst of a devastating storm at sea. Their boat was sinking. Jesus was in the boat sleeping. Imagine being in that boat—your Savior appearing indifferent to the turmoil. Sometimes, with all that is going on in the world, we wonder if God is asleep, if He is aware of what's going on. Yet, like the disciples in the boat, all we need to do is call on Him, and He will be there in our time of trouble. Jesus calmed the wind and the waves.

Even Peter, the same Peter who would deny Jesus, could count on Jesus. He was able to walk on the water as long as he kept his eyes on Jesus and not the waves. You see, it wasn't about Peter's perfection, but about overcoming fear with faith, which is the confidence that God is who He says He is and will not let you sink.

These stories apply to our lives. When we accept Jesus through the salvation prayer, things shift. Mountains move, storms cease, and healing begins. Recognizing that Jesus is in the boat of our lives, our worries dissipate, and the waters of our existence become calm. As we await the rapture, there's no need to fear; He is in control. Embrace His joy, abide in the Almighty, and everything will be all right in the waiting period.

Wrap-up: Through divine messages and anticipation of the rapture, God initiates communication with us, guiding us with hope and preparing us for His return.

Reflective Questions:

How do you discern divine messages or symbols from God in your life?

In what ways does the anticipation of Christ's return impact your perspective on life and faith?

9

Peace Be Still!

In the journey to become who I am, my mother played a significant role by being a beacon of creativity and intelligence. She possessed a remarkable ability to breathe life into things. For example, she could transform an ordinary piece of fabric into something wonderous. It was her passion, so she taught it to me. Creating garments was a skill I acquired. However, as much as I appreciated the art of sewing and creating beautiful things, I sensed that it wasn't my medium to work with. Recognizing my need for vibrant self-expression, my mother redirected my focus towards art classes. Painting became a canvas for my colorful imagination; a realm where I could give life to the kaleidoscope of thoughts swirling within me. It did not stop there. Dance, too, became another outlet for my artistic and boundless energy. The thought of being still gave me discomfort. I had to be moving all the time. I craved movement, and that transferred into her areas of my life. I took that energy and used it for the onstant pursuit of goals to accomplish anything and everything. The idea of being still and waiting on the Lord was a aunting idea, especially in the midst of storms in my life. I mply did not know how to do it and was at odds with myself because I saw many times in the Bible where the Lord said e wanted me to have peace and calm in my life. One of the ost well-known scriptures that refers to a storm is in Mark. he disciples were in a boat fishing when a storm arose, and ley immediately began to be afraid and have anxiety over hat might happen to them. They woke Jesus and he handled ne storm for them.

Then He arose and rebuked the wind, and said to the sea, "Peace, be still!" And the wind ceased and there was a great calm. (Mark 4:39 NKJV)

There was not only calm in the sea but in the hearts and linds of the disciples. This is not the only time God tells his eople to be at peace. Here are several other scriptures.

So, the Levites quieted all the people, saying, "Be still, for the day is holy; do not be grieved. (Nehemiah 8:11 NKJV)

Be angry, and do not sin. Meditate within your heart on your bed and be still. Selah. (Psalm 4:4 NKJV)

Be still and know that I am God; I will be exalted among the nations, I will be exalted in the earth! (Psalm 46:10 NKJV)

Although the Bible is clear on being still in the storms
life, it was a daunting challenge for me. When God, in H
wisdom, urged me to be still and wait, my immediate r
action was resistance. I saw it as a clash with my very natur
a potential disaster. I couldn't fathom the concept of waitin
It contradicted the essence of who I believed I was. Yet, God
call to stillness wasn't a mere suggestion. It was a divine i
struction to transform my ways for His higher purpose.

One day I was listening to a beautiful song by Hope Dars
with the fitting name, "Peace Be Still." The lyrics of the son
express a powerful message about overcoming fear and fin
ing tranquility in the middle of life's challenges. The sing
acknowledges the power and presence of God in the midd
of the storm. The singer encourages the hearer to stand stron
and firm in faith and surrender your circumstances to th
Lord. The lyrics poured over me like a wave and my min
wandered. I began to reflect on the many storms I was facin
in my own life. I had problems in my business, my person
life, my husband had been diagnosed with cancer and eve
my sons were having troubles. I am not an excuse maker; I an
a doer, but all of this at once was simply overwhelming. I wa
definitely in the middle of a storm. I wanted to do somethin
It is my nature, but what could I do? I am a natural bor
leader. I love to lead and teach, and I felt that all eyes wer
on me to have the answers. So, I went to the Lord, and H
said, "Peace be still." It did not make sense to me at the time
but now I see that every storm was an opportunity for Go
to speak into my life. It was not easy. As I embarked on thi
unfamiliar journey of stillness, I grappled with internal strug
gles. My restlessness manifested as anxiety, panic attacks, an

emotions I found difficult to control. The discipline of being still was tormenting, and sometimes seemed like self-imposed torture that I had chosen to inflict upon myself. But let me assure you, in the midst of this internal chaos, God's voice began to penetrate the noise.

The silence that accompanied stillness became a training ground for my soul. In the absence of external distractions, I started to hear the subtle whispers of His voice. The tornado of my thoughts, like a blender on overdrive, began to settle into stillness. God was orchestrating a symphony in the quietude, teaching me the art of listening.

God is referred to as "Elohim" in the Bible which means "The Creator" who breathed life into humanity. He created us perfectly. However, he also gave us a choice to make our own decisions. We can make good ones or bad ones. The bible is a specific set of instructions on how to line up with the best that God has for us. Sometimes our freedom of choice in life can lead to worldly confusion. The ways outside of God are deceitful and we can get lost. In other words, when we take it all into our own hands it can lead to an even bigger mess and inner harm.

God Has a Good Plan

I struggled as a single mother of two sons. I suffered from anxiety. I had panic attacks. The stress of being the only provider for my sons was enormous. I did not understand why the answers I was looking for took so long. Sometimes I had no one I could count on, and the only one I could go to was Jesus. We do not understand sometimes why our plans do not work out, and we try producing a plan "B." Plan "B" is a plan that we design ourselves without consulting God. I was an impatient person. I wanted my answer, and I wanted it now! I began to pray for God to help me be patient. I began to do less planning and more listening to what God had to say to me either through his word in the Bible or through pastors or even through the still quiet voice of the Holy Spirit. God began to reveal to me that every answer He had for me was time-framed. Each thing that God had for me was supposed to happen at a particular time. We can see God's timing in everything in the universe. Developing patience is an art. It means to let go and let God; let go of our plans and let Him lead. He has a perfect plan; it's balanced and geared to meet your needs. While you wait on God, get yourself lined up with His purpose for you. Search it out and pursue it. When we get in alignment with God, the answer He gives us is yes and amen. God gives us each the freedom to choose. If we choose our way and not His, we reap the fruit of our choices. Know that God's plan is a good one. It will make you happy and meet your needs, above and beyond what you could ever imagine in your plan "B."

Wrap-up: By embracing stillness in the storm and maintaining faith in adversity, God takes the initiative to offer peace and hope, inviting us to trust Him amid life's challenges.

Reflective Questions:

How do you embrace stillness and find peace in the midst of life's storms and uncertainties?

Reflect on a time when your faith sustained you through adversity. What lessons did you learn about trusting God?

10

The Drama Button

I remember a television commercial by TNT which featured a drama button in the middle of the street. It sat there beckoning anyone to push the big red button which had an arrow with the words "Push here to add drama." One man on a bike comes by and pauses, looks around, and decides to push the button. Then all matters of chaos break loose. Ambulances, fist fights, gun fights, accidents, all manners of drama ensue, and the crowd watches in awe as it all plays out. Well, in this world, there are all kinds of influences, and we have an enemy who loves to press the DRAMA button! How we choose to deal with it changes everything. God says to give our troubles to him. Peace be Still. Only God can stop the drama. He gives us this promise in His word.

A thousand may fall at your side, and ten thousand at your right hand. But it shall not come near you. Only with your eyes shall you look and see the reward of the wicked. (Psalm 91:7-8 NKJV)

Sometimes when we are in a place of submission to God there are lots of things going on in the spiritual world that we cannot see. Many times, there is chaos and drama we cannot foresee being prevented from happening. Angels are in the midst fighting on our behalf.

Twenty-one Day Fast

One way to be still is to practice fasting and praying. I recall the story of Daniel where archangels were fighting to answer Daniel's prayer unbeknownst to Daniel who was in waiting. They fought for 21 days! Let's read the story.

In the third year of Cyrus, king of Persia, a message was revealed to Daniel, whose name was called Belteshazzar. The message was true, but the appointed time was long; and he understood the message and understood the vision. In those days I, Daniel, was mourning three full weeks. I ate no pleasant food, no meat or wine came into my mouth, nor did I anoint myself at all, till three whole weeks were fulfilled.

Now on the twenty-fourth day of the first month, as I was by the side of the great river, that is, the Tigris, I lifted my eyes and looked, and behold, a certain man clothed in linen, whose waist was girded with gold of Uphaz! His body was like beryl, his face like the appearance of lightning, his eyes like torches of fire, his arms, and feet like burnished bronze in color, and the sound of

*his words like the voice of a multitude. And I, Daniel, alone saw
the vision, for the men who were with me did not see the vision;
but a great terror fell upon them, so that they fled to hide themselves. Therefore I was left alone when I saw this great vision,
and no strength remained in me; for my vigor was turned to
frailty in me, and I retained no strength. Yet I heard the sound
of his words; and while I heard the sound of his words I was in a
deep sleep on my face, with my face to the ground.*

*Suddenly, a hand touched me, which made me tremble on my
knees and on the palms of my hands. And he said to me, "O
Daniel, man greatly beloved, understand the words that I speak
to you, and stand upright, for I have now been sent to you."
While he was speaking this word to me, I stood trembling. Then
he said to me, "Do not fear, Daniel, for from the first day that
you set your heart to understand, and to humble yourself before
your God, your words were heard; and I have come because of
your words. But the prince of the kingdom of Persia withstood me
twenty-one days; and behold, Michael, one of the chief princes,
came to help me, for I had been left alone there with the kings
of Persia. Now I have come to make you understand what will
happen to your people in the latter days, for the vision refers to
many days yet to come."*

*When he had spoken such words to me, I turned my face toward
the ground and became speechless. And suddenly, one having the
likeness of the sons of men touched my lips; then I opened my
mouth and spoke, saying to him who stood before me, "My lord,
because of the vision my sorrows have overwhelmed me, and I
have retained no strength. For how can this servant of my lord*

talk with you, my lord? As for me, no strength remains in me now, nor is any breath left in me."

Then again, the one having the likeness of a man touched me and strengthened me. And he said, "O man greatly beloved, fear not! Peace be to you; be strong, yes, be strong!"

So, when he spoke to me, I was strengthened, and said, "Let my lord speak, for you have strengthened me."

Then he said, "Do you know why I have come to you? And now I must return to fight with the prince of Persia; and when I have gone forth, indeed the prince of Greece will come. But I will tell you what is noted in the Scripture of Truth. (No one upholds me against these, except Michael your prince.

(Daniel 10:1-21 NKJV)

Take note. The decision to fast for 21 days wasn't Daniel's idea, and it has deep meaning in our spiritual battles. When we fast for 21 days, we grow where we would not usually grow, and we become stronger and wiser. This chapter concludes with an awe-inspiring 21st verse, emphasizing the significance of a 21-day period of fasting. This duration represents the time required to achieve victory over the principalities and powers of darkness that sought to obstruct the answers to the prayers of God's people. On the 21st day, God dispatched the archangel Michael to assist Daniel in receiving the answers to his prayers.

Whenever God's conflict with the demonic hosts of heaven is described, the archangel Michael is summoned to defeat the enemies of God. The choice of a 21-day fast was not made by Daniel; rather, it was ordained by God and holds significant spiritual warfare symbolism.

Fasting for 21 days holds a special significance as it is a time when God connects with His people in a unique way. During this period, a divine power enters the life of a believer, bringing about a transformation. It's more than just acknowledging that the archangel Michael fought and won against our enemies; even after the fast, he continues to battle on our behalf.

The 21 days of fasting become a crucial time for receiving answers to our prayers. This dedicated period also opens the door to new revelations and a deeper understanding of God's Word. I found this insight intriguing when I explored the concept of the 21 days of prayer in the book of Daniel. Fasting serves as a powerful tool, breaking the chains the enemy may have placed on our lives.

In my own journey, the 21-day fast marked the beginning of a remarkable work of God in my life. In a season of brokenness, similar to the jewelry metaphor I shared earlier, God utilized the stillness to initiate a profound transformation. The once-feared silence became a sanctuary, allowing me to discern His voice and receive the much-needed guidance for my soul.

In embracing the stillness, I discovered a profound truth: my identity wasn't solely defined by constant motion and achievement. God's call to "be still" became a pathway to healing and restoration. It marked the initiation of a divine process that would mend the broken pieces of my being and shape me into the person He intended me to be.

Praying For Patience

As I said before, being a single mother taught me to pray! It taught me to depend on God. It also taught me to pray for patience and to become patient. Some of you think that you do not have any patience. Did you know that you can pray for patience? I recall one day that Jesus came to me and spoke in a still, small calm voice in my ear. So, I want to give you this prayer.

"Jesus come to me, speak your calm words in my ears. Let me hear your calm voice and let your words pour into the spirit of my heart. Let your light touch my soul. Come and calm my heart. Make me be patient, Lord. In my waiting on you, let me have your peace once again. Heal all of my sorrows. Let your heavenly light shine bright on me as I wait. Let me have peace in waiting for the solution. Give me Peace. Amen."

Rejoice in hope, be patient in tribulation, be constant in prayer. (Romans 12:12 ESV)

Patience is an art that matures with time and experience. It involves a shift from impulsive "plan Bs" to a patient alignment with God's plans. Although we have the freedom to choose our paths, opting for our own plans may prolong our journey.

So, as we face the complexities of life, let's trade our impatience for the peace that comes with waiting on Jesus. The journey may seem to take longer, but the destination is more beautiful than we could ever imagine.

Wrap-up: Through embracing stillness in the midst of spiritual warfare, God initiates a process of inner strength and victory, equipping us to overcome fear and adversity.

Reflective Questions:

How do you overcome the enemy in the midst of spiritual warfare with faith in your daily life?

What should you keep your eyes on when you are in the middle of a storm and overcome with Fear?

Reflect on a time when you experienced victory over spiritual battles through prayer and faith. What strategies did you use to overcome? how can you use them in your daily life?

True Believers

When I was younger, I embarked on a journey to explore various religions, seeking to understand who God is and where He exists. My quest led me from Christianity to spiritualism, Buddhism and even witchcraft. In Brazil, I encountered a unique blend of Catholicism mixed with the African culture where gods were represented by Catholic saints in a practice known as spiritualism or Umbanda. Umanda is a mix of cultural and religious influences.

Key tenants of Umbanda include:

1. Syncretism: Umbanda incorporates deities and spirits from various traditions. The entities worshiped in Umbanda often have counterparts in Catholicism, such as saints.

2. Mediumship: Umbanda places a strong emphasis on communication with spirits. Mediums are individuals believed to have the ability to communicate with the spirit world. During ceremonies, these mediums may enter trance states and allow spirits to manifest through them.

3. Spiritual Hierarchy: Umbanda recognizes a hierarchy of spirits, entities known as "Orixás" (associated with Yoruba deities), guides, and protectors. Each spirit may have a specific role and is called upon for different purposes.

4. Rituals and Ceremonies: Umbanda ceremonies involve music, dance, and offerings to the orixás. Participants seek spiritual guidance, healing, and protection during these rituals. Offerings may include candles, flowers, and food.

5. Catholic Influence: Umbanda incorporates Catholic elements, such as the use of saints and symbols, which reflects the historical influence of Catholicism in Brazil.

6. Magical Practices: Practitioners of Umbanda may engage in magical practices, including the use of herbs, charms, and rituals for spiritual and physical well being.

During my involvement in this religion, I served as an assistant, witnessing rituals and experiencing the manifestation of spirits through individuals. Surprisingly, in the midst of his spiritual exploration, despite me going the wrong direction, God did not give up on me. God spoke to me, conveying a message that He allowed me to delve into these beliefs to discern the difference between true belief in Him verses other entities. Despite my worship of different gods, God remained by my side, granting me the freedom to explore, and this experience led me to understand the difference between false gods and false religions and to appreciate Him as the one true living God of the universe.

One evening, when I was getting ready to attend, God held me back, whispering, "Don't go; it won't be good for you." Despite trying to disobey, an unseen force kept me inside my house. I felt God's hands insistently preventing my departure. My mother, a Christian, questioned me twice, asking if I was going that day. I explained to her the strange feeling I had, and the voice telling me not to go. I chose not to attend. The following day, a friend informed me that another assistant had suffered severe burns in an accidental fire at the place I was supposed to be. I felt deep sympathy for her, but I recognized God's protective hand, guiding me to stay home that particular evening. It could have been me in that unfortunate incident, but God shielded me, and I obeyed His prompting to stay safe. This incident marked the end of my involvement in that spiritual path. Later in life, I saw this scripture which also confirmed the falseness of this religion.

> Do not turn to mediums or necromancers; do not seek them out, and so make yourselves unclean by them: I am the Lord your God. (Leviticus 19:31 ESV)

My quest for spiritual knowledge continued, leading me to explore a type of Buddhism practiced by my younger sister. The teachings involved the imposition of energy through hands, and I found it intriguing. However, as I delved deeper, I discovered that they worshipped forty-eight different gods and believed in the reincarnation of human spirits into animals.

So, what did I learn in all of this exploring? There is only one God, true and powerful, creator of the universe, who became a man named Jesus, who gave himself for the redemption of our sins and the clearing of eternal damnation through belief, repentance, and the confession of our mouth that He is Lord of all! God revealed to me that even in my disobedience He loves me and has protected me. I now understand that not all religions lead to the one true living God, and that Satan often distorts the true identity of God. The Bible declares there is no other God; there is only one true God. Despite hearing people claim that all religions lead to the same God, my search for God revealed that not all gods are the same. The Bible is the inspired word of God, written by men inspired by God. The Bible says that God's word is true, does not lie and clearly communicates the uniqueness of the Almighty.

As I explored these paths, God in his grace granted me the freedom to seek and learn, leading me back to Him. His love and patience allowed me to mature in my faith, recognizing that there is none like Him. I would like to call your attention to some Bible verses that reinforce the truth that there is none like the Lord, and His greatness is unmatched.

Inasmuch as there is none like You, O Lord (You are great, and Your name is great in might). (Jeremiah 10:6 NKJV)

No one is holy like the Lord, for there is none besides You, nor is there any rock like our God. (1 Samuel 2:2 NKJV)

O Lord, there is none like You, nor is there any God besides You, according to all that we have heard with our ears. (1 Chronicles 17:20 NKJV)

There is no one like the God of Jeshurun, who rides the heavens to help you, and in His excellency on the clouds. (Deuteronomy 33:26 NKJV)

So, he said, 'Tomorrow.' And he said, 'Let it be according to your word, that you may know that there is no one like the Lord our God.' (Exodus 8:10 NKJV)

'for at this time I will send all My plagues to your very heart, and on your servants and on your people, that you may know that there is none like Me in all the earth.' (Exodus 9:14 NKJV)

O Lord God, You have begun to show Your servant Your greatness and Your mighty hand, for what god is there in heaven or on earth who can do anything like Your works and Your mighty deeds? (Deuteronomy 3:24 NKJV)

And he said: 'Lord God of Israel, there is no God in heaven above or on earth below like You, who keeps Your covenant and mercy with Your servants who walk before You with all their hearts.' (1 Kings 8:23 NKJV)

Therefore, You are great, O Lord God. For there is none like You, nor is there any God besides You, according to all that we have heard with our ears. (2 Samuel 7:22 NKJV)

Among the gods there is none like You, O Lord; nor are there any works like Your works. (Psalm 86:8 NKJV)

Don't Believe a Lie

I've encountered individuals who believe that God is universally the same across all religions, with various paths leading to the same divine entity under different names. However, I can personally attest that these diverse gods are not the one true God. The Bible consistently emphasizes not believing in such gods, as God has rebuked them.

You shall have no other gods before Me. You shall not make for yourself a carved image—any likeness of anything that is in heaven above, or that is in the earth beneath, or that is in the water under the earth; you shall not bow down to them nor serve them. (Exodus 20:3-4 NKJV)

The Gift

God has uniquely placed a special seed within each of us. During our upbringing, our parents guide us to pursue goals and purposes through various educational paths, including school and apprenticeships. There are diverse avenues for learning and growth. I vividly recall my father's desire for me to enter the field of medicine. While it might have been a

ore conventional choice, it didn't resonate with the creative
assion within me. I firmly believe when God plants a seed in
for a specific purpose, it becomes our calling. True peace
ad happiness emerge when we wholeheartedly pursue what
od has placed within us.

In my case, I chose cosmetology, a decision which aligned
ith my artistic nature. This path allowed me to express my
ove for beauty and art, tapping into natural talents that were
inherent to me. Cosmetology provided the perfect platform
to channel my artistic abilities, offering fulfillment and a
ense of purpose in my chosen career. God has a calling for
ach individual. He begins and refines the training process
throughout their life, culminating in experiences and learning until a divine point, a sort of graduation. There are no
limitations on what one can or cannot do with God. In fact,
God has a special love for problematic or imperfect individuals. He knows just who to utilize for what purpose and can
se anyone at any stage of their life. Someone who needs God
may only trust a certain type of person to teach them. I have
often seen people on motorcycles with tattoos and became
scared, only to realize after talking to them, they were in
fact pastors and evangelists out in the world spreading the
good news about how God had transformed them. When
God transforms our lives, the transformation brings about
significant changes and releases a powerful river of anointing
that affects the world around us. People who have experienced rough times in their lives truly understand the grace of
God and the process it takes to be purified and made a new
creation in Christ.

God envisions a future focused on the prosperity of the

soul and the manifestation of the fruits of the Spirit; lov
joy, peace, patience, kindness, goodness, faithfulness, gentl
ness, and self-control (Galatians 5). As we develop the frui
of the Spirit, we undergo a spiritual transformation. Th
shift results in lives that are less bound to earthly concern
leading to reduced worries, increased peace, a calm spiri
and a peaceful mind. This transformation brings about holi
tic benefits, including improved health, discernment, and
secure understanding of one's identity in Christ. When face
with adversity, individuals with developed spiritual frui
know how to navigate challenges and respond in alignmer
with their faith.

There were many prophets in the Bible, men of God wh
prophesied God's truth. They did not bring the truth to fru
tion themselves but allowed God's people to understand tha
God is in the plans He has for them, and things happen fc
a reason. If you have an ear hear, then hear. The Bible says i
John 10:27, "*My sheep hear My voice, and I know them, and the
follow Me. And I give them eternal life...*" (NKJV).

When these prophets spoke, what they said happened
Even today there are people who have been given the gift c
prophesy to be used to keep God's people on track. Althoug
I do not have the gift of prophesy, God has made a way t
reveal to me many things that He has for me to do in my life
Keep your ears attentive and your eyes open to the peopl
God has placed in your life and to the things which God i
showing you from His word, so you may know the plans Go
has for you and seek after them. We are coming into an age c
miracles where even children with their child-like faith wi
operate in the power of God. In these last days we will se

signs and wonders. Remember the devil is a counterfeit. He will also perform signs and wonders. Therefore, stay close to the Lord so that you may discern the difference. Signs and wonders from God glorify God so that those who experience them may know who God is and be saved.

Wrap-up: Desiree's personal experience validates the existence of the one true living God, particularly during the transformative night when she touched Jesus. In that profound encounter, numerous truths were revealed to her. She can confidently assert that Jesus Christ stands as the sole God in Heaven capable of transforming lives, healing the sick, and forgiving sins. It is crucial not to succumb to the manipulations of Satan. As she began to listen and obey God, a remarkable change unfolded. The areas of her life that were in disarray and the aspects within her that needed transformation underwent a profound and lasting change. This transformation serves as a testament to the power of the one true living God in bringing about positive and lasting change.

Reflective Questions:

What characteristics define a true believer in your opinion? How do you strive to embody those qualities in your life?

Reflect on the gift of salvation and its significance in your faith journey. How does knowing you have eternal life impact the way you live?

12

The Cure

It's hard to live in the fullness of all God has for you if you do not know that you need healing. We may get used to the symptoms and downplay them as a normal part of existence. There may truly be symptoms that are plaguing us, but we keep them because it's all that we have ever known. Take being thirsty. If you have always been thirsty then you wouldn't know the benefits of what it's like not to be. The journey to healing begins with an acknowledgment of our inherent need for it; whether it's an affliction of your physical body or an affliction of your soul. There is also an inter-connectedness of body, spirit, and soul which plays a pivotal role in the outcome. Your spirit is a gateway for all things spiritual; negative or positive. If you are not on guard spiritually and lined up with the Holy Spirit, then evil influences may creep in. This opens the door to demonic manipulation, spiritual and physical disobedience, anger, jealousy, envy, and

·confusion, all collectively working to shatter what I refer to as God's masterpiece, 'The Original Creation.' We start out pure and perfect. Then the enemy seeks to keep us from looking like the image of God, and instead deceives us to look and act like him and suffer his destiny of being separated from God for eternity.

It is not the enemy alone per se, but he loves to be an influencer. I believe that our surroundings—be it the environment, family, friends, or the spiritual realm—exert a profound influence on us throughout our lives. We, though, make our own decisions.

Above all else, guard your heart, for everything you do flows from it. (Proverbs 4:23 NIV)

Even if you grew up in perfect familial and educational settings, it is the absence of God's presence that can significantly impact your spiritual well-being. The devil and his influencers are after one thing, your soul. If that means attacking you to the point where you believe that God doesn't exist, then they will. This spiritual assault can manifest itself in your life in the forms of depression, oppression, and even possession. Mental disorders, unbalanced souls, and disease become the aftermath. Hidden principalities and powers work on behalf of Satan to wreak havoc on our lives, our families, our businesses, and our physical health, all with one purpose - to erode our belief in a caring God who is simply waiting for the prayers of believers to triumph over the forces of darkness in this world.

Without our alignment with God through Jesus, the enemy

an attack. Spiritual sickness aims to rupture our belief in a loving God. When in fact, God is always there for us, overseeing our lives.

Generational Curses

A Generational Curse is a sickness or symptom that gets passed down generationally. It could be in the form of a lie or a physical sickness. We have all heard someone say, "Well, I have that because it runs in my family." Or we have seen what seems like a coincidence that strikes family generations over and over again, as if each generation carried a magnet that attracted this terrible thing to happen to them. These negative spirits can perpetuate their influence across generations, passing down the symptoms of the enemy from one generation to the next. However, because of Christ, we have the authority to break generational curses. I have witnessed individuals delivered from such curses and have been a testament to the transformative power of spiritual intervention.

I recall a personal experience with a friend who volunteers in deliverance meetings. He conducted a session for a young woman in my husband's family grappling with severe spiritual issues including hearing voices which were urging her to self-harm. The prayers proved effective, leading to her mental and spiritual freedom from the spirit of death.

Some people experience deliverance instantaneously, and for others it takes time. While the journey to freedom may not be instantaneous, the length of its duration often correlates with the damage inflicted by the spiritual affliction. The Bible also says you can be set free, but if you go back into your sin,

that you have only cleaned your spiritual house to allow mor
trouble to move back in. Therefore, repentance and turnin
away from sin and to Christ's ways is essential. The enem
will not leave you alone if you willfully walk into his camp. I
also underscores the potential for relapse if repentance and
return to the Lord Jesus Christ are not embraced. Therefor
walking with God is the essential component for a joyful an
healthy life.

Why Do Christians Get Attacked?

A lingering question persists: why do some Christians fac
demonic attacks? We are at war with a real enemy. The answe
to this lies in faith. When we genuinely believe in God
ability, and have unwavering faith, He intervenes to delive
healing. The removal of obsessive spirits from the heart an
soul occurs through prayer, where the acceptance of God
intervention with repentance reaches deep into our spirit
The infusion of God's light into our souls signifies a renewa
of our original form—a rebirth in Him. Impurities of sin ar
expelled, and we become free from the spiritual bondage
that once ensnared us. Yet, the susceptibility to spiritual at
tacks persists, fueled by sin, doubt, and thoughts that oppos
Christ. Despite our human weaknesses, God, in His forgivin
nature, cleanses and forgives us when we confess our sins t
Him. We, as "sons and daughters of God," are part of Hi
creation, and His presence is with us.

Healing is a tangible reality. God awaits our plea for heal
ing, urging us to believe in His ability. While the process ma
take time, the key lies in our faith. Instead of dwelling on th

"why," let us embrace a steadfast belief in His name, where miracles have occurred and will continue to unfold.

My Mind, His Control

As I delved into my Bible, a powerful revelation emerged from 2 Corinthians 10:5: *"We demolish arguments and every pretension that sets itself against the knowledge of God, and we take captive every thought to make it obedient to Christ."* (NIV). This profound statement struck a chord within me, signifying the power of aligning our thoughts with the wisdom and knowledge of God. Disobedience, in the context of this verse, is the result of thoughts diverging from God's words. It's a rebellion against His rules and regulations, leading to internal conflict and confusion. When we empower ourselves outside of God's wisdom, we distance ourselves from His deep knowledge and goodness. The remedy lies in surrender. God simply asks us to pray and believe, entrusting Him with our desires and dreams. We need not fight battles alone; His angels are ready to assist. The battle against conflicting thoughts and worries is not ours alone.

In prayer, we can cast out worries and conflicting thoughts. Acknowledging our inability to solve problems independently, we surrender our minds to God's control. The process involves recognizing that attempting to be our own gods only leads to confusion and distance from God's perfect love.

One thing God asks us to do is to PRAY and BELIEVE. Call on Him. Give it all to him; your hopes, desires, and dreams. He knows you. He knows what you're overcoming. If you lean on Him, He will not leave you alone in the battle.

Remember that He has an angel army for just this purpose. Jesus knows what you need!

Let's pray for all worries and wrong thoughts to be cast out! Your prayer might go something like this:

"Jesus, I have become tired thinking about this problem over and over! I know you are able to clear my thoughts and free me from this worry, and I know these are problems I cannot solve myself. Jesus, I can't do anything without you. Please clean up my mind and free me from any thoughts the enemy put before me to stumble on. Lord, take captive every thought that is unpleasing to you. I am resisting the enemy, therefore, don't let the enemy have control over me. I'm submitting every thought. Lead me, Lord. Thank you, Lord! My thoughts are free now in the name of Jesus! Amen"

Wrap-up: Through the cure for spiritual ailments and God's good plan, God initiates a process of restoration and purpose, offering hope and direction in our lives.

Reflective Questions:

How do you seek spiritual healing and restoration in areas of brokenness or weakness?

In what ways do you trust God's good plan for your life, even in the midst of uncertainty or adversity?

13

Unmasking Deception and Seeking Truth in a World of Lies

To the Jews who had believed him, Jesus said, "If you hold to my teaching, you are really my disciples. Then you will know the truth, and the truth will set you free." (John 8:31-32 NKJV)

In today's world, trust is a scarce commodity, as the age-old adage states "all lies beneath" resonates more than ever. The inherent deceitfulness of human nature is acknowledged and expressed in Psalm 116:11, which states, "*I said in my haste, 'All men are liars.'*" (NKJV).

This acknowledgment, however, does not astonish, as lies in this world, no matter how pretty or profound, have become a common occurrence. I remember when my kids were

ttle. Occasionally, they would lie to me. I would inevitably
ee it in their eyes. Their perception was that I was not going
to like what it was they were trying to hide. Their perception
was right. I am sure they remember my flip flops flying across
the room in their direction. My point being that I did not
teach them to lie. Lying came naturally to them. Just like I
knew with my children when they told lies, God knows even
more so! Thus, our attempts to conceal them are futile.

Telling the truth was once encouraged because of moral
standards. But the scales are tipping. The world seems to lean
into lying, and the problem is getting worse. Reflecting on
the prevalent misinformation rampant in the world, today's
"truth" is like a candle that is swayed by public opinion. The
goal of people who have been persuaded by the enemy is to do
everything they can to sway public opinion and create a new
false truth. The more something is said, the more it seems
true. But it is not truth. You only have to switch channels,
listen to the news, and hear the many versions of the so-called
"truth;" each network spinning the story of what happened
in its own way. A world built on deception has a shaky foun-
dation, and it will affect generations. Adolf Hitler's Minister
of Propaganda, Joseph Goebells, stated this, "If you tell a lie
long enough, it becomes the truth."

Yet, in the midst of all of these falsehoods, there is hope
for the world if we follow Jesus. Jesus epitomizes truth and
challenges the web of lies. So, what is the truth that we
should know about? Jesus, creator of the universe, brought a
message of love for all humanity. His teachings transcended
boundaries, embracing people of diverse backgrounds, political affiliations, and religious beliefs. We are called to love one

another and follow God with all of our heart, soul, and mind. We are called to lead others to the truth and teach them about Jesus and set the captives free.

> *Therefore go and make disciples of all nations, baptizing them in the name of the Father and the Son and of the Holy Spirit, and teaching them to obey everything I have commanded you. And surely I am with you always, to the very end of the age.* (Matthew 28:19-20 NIV)

This call extends to believers, urging them to share the transformative truth found in the Holy Trinity.

God Leads to the Truth in All Things

There is timeless wisdom to be found in the book of Isaiah relating to God as our ultimate guide and that He is the source of our existence. We have all heard the saying, "There is nothing new under the sun." The book of Isaiah parallels modern times, and therefore is relevant to us today.

In the book of Isaiah, the Lord talks to the people of Israel, saying He's their creator and the source of their life. He emphasizes that He rescued them and created everything around them. Even though these words were written a long time ago, they still hold power and can relate to what's happening in our world today.

Isaiah describes how the people turned away from God's commandments, started believing in other gods, and faced corruption. The country ended up in ruins, much like what Isaiah says in another part about towns lying in ashes and oreigners taking over the land. This might sound familiar when we look at what's on the news today – when people urn away from God, it can lead to chaos and problems.

Isaiah 44:24-28 (CEV) says, "*Israel, I am your Lord, the source f your life, and I have rescued you. I created everything from the ky above to the earth below.*"

Isaiah 1:7 (CEV) adds, "*Your country lies in ruins; your towns ire in ashes. Foreigners and strangers take and destroy your land vhile you watch.*" Interestingly, Isaiah also talks about Cyrus, someone chosen by God to do His work, even though Cyrus night not have known God personally.

Isaiah 45:1-7 (CEV) records God saying, "*I have made you strong, though you don't know me. Now everyone from east to west vill learn that I am the Lord. No other gods are real.*"

This shows that God can use different people for His plans. God's message is clear: He is there as our guiding light, even when things seem confusing. When people stray from God's path, it leads to trouble. This chapter emphasizes the need to stay close to God, acknowledge Him as the one in charge, and avoid false beliefs. It's about understanding that our lives are connected to God, and without Him, we're missing our true identity and purpose.

Wrap-up: God unmasks deception through His leadership. God initiates a journey of truth and guidance, inviting us to discern His will and follow Him faithfully.

Reflective Questions:

How do you discern truth from deception in a world filled with lies and distractions?

Reflect on a time when you felt God's leading and guidance in your life. How did you respond to His direction?

Knowing what you know now would you have done something different? If so, what?

14

Passion for Christ

Have you ever thought about what true happiness and love really mean? It seems like everyone is searching for them, but sometimes we end up looking in all the wrong places. There's a country song that says, "I was looking for love in the wrong places," and it got me thinking. We're all investing our time and energy in things that won't bring us lasting joy. The Bible talks about enjoying life and finding joy in our toil. Ecclesiastes 8:15 (NIV) says, "*So I commend the enjoyment of life because there is nothing better for a person under the sun than to eat, drink, and be glad. Then joy will accompany them in their toil all the days of the life God has given them under the sun.*" The phrase "under the sun" means here on earth, where we are right now.

We often find ourselves unsatisfied, comparing our lives to others, wanting more, and thinking that the grass is greener on the other side. Our consumerist mentality comes from a disposable world and the "I must have it now" mindset.

This is why we end up searching for love in the wrong places. The things we pursue don't satisfy us because they are temporary. Our passions, those intense feelings we have at the start of a relationship, fade away. That's why it's crucial to understand the difference between passion and real love.

I discovered true love and ongoing happiness when I started loving Jesus deeply and putting Him first above everything and everyone. It wasn't an instant transformation. It took a lifetime of working on myself. When Jesus showed up in my life, His love went beyond any feeling I had ever experienced. True love and happiness are simple yet complicated. It depends on how you view love. I found that nothing can ruin my day when I prioritize the love and happiness found in Jesus. When I do this, other things lose their significance. It doesn't mean you won't have good things in life, but they take a back seat to Him. The Bible says, "*To the person who pleases Him, God gives wisdom, knowledge, and happiness, but to the sinner, He gives the task of gathering and storing up wealth to hand it over to the one who pleases God. This too is meaningless, a chasing after the wind.*" (Ecclesiastes 2:26, NIV) It also states when you find delight in the Lord, He gives you the desires of your heart (Psalms 37:4).

In relationships, putting God above everything allows things to flow in the right direction. The center becomes Him, not your spouse or family or friends.

So, as you navigate life, remember that true happiness and love are found in Jesus, not in the fleeting passions of the world.

The Tree of Everlasting Life

I love movies, one particular movie is the movie Avatar. Have you ever watched a movie so many times that you just can't get enough of it? For me, that movie is Avatar. But it's not just about cool visuals and epic battles; there's a deeper meaning that I discovered, and it's all about connection.

In the movie the main character, Jake Sully, undergoes a spiritual transformation as he embraces the ways of the Na'vi people's spiritual beliefs. As Jake immerses himself in Na'vi culture, he undergoes a transformation. Falling in love with Neytiri, a Na'vi princess, he gradually distances himself from the human military agenda. The turning point comes when Jake connects spiritually with the Na'vi's sacred Tree of Souls. The Tree of Souls is reminiscent of the Tree of Life in the Garden of Eden, symbolizing a spiritual link between the Na'vi and their deity, Eywa. Jake's connection to this sacred tree signifies a deep embrace of Na'vi spirituality and a rejection of human exploitation.

In Avatar, the natives hold something dear – "The Tree." It's not just any tree; it's like their life source. Whenever they face problems or get sick, they connect with this special tree, which is a nurturing god-type figure. They seek answers, and it becomes clear that this tree is their key to life.

There is also a scene in the movie that introduces what look like floating seeds. One of these seeds seems to choose Jake, the main character. This signifies to the Na'vi people that Jake is chosen and is considered special to Eywa and to the Na'vi way of life. This got me thinking. God showed me similar concept, the tree of life God placed in paradise.

In the beginning, Adam and Eve were connected to Go through a tree. It represented God's power, love, and al knowing wisdom. Whenever they wanted to talk to Goc they went to this tree. The connection was so powerful tha nothing could take away God's presence, except one thing – broken promise, a disobedience to God's command (Genes 2:17). Because of this disobedience we were disconnected fror God. However, God sent his seed to choose us. Enter Jesus the Seed that connects us to God, the ultimate source of lif He was sent to be our connection to God, an intercesso making the way for us to connect with God our Heavenl father. Jesus said, *"I am the way, and the truth, and the life. N one comes to the Father except through me."* (John 14:6 NIV) tree comes from a seed, and a seed comes from the tree. tree bears fruit. The fruits of the Spirit are born from thi connection.

Now, picture paradise with another magnificent tree radiating the knowledge of good and evil. The most beautifu tempting fruit hangs from its branches as well, giving us th choice too of knowing everything. But God said that it woul not be good for us, for it is an invitation, a temptatior to know more than we should. God gives us the choice t choose the tree of life but shows us the tree of knowledge o good and evil. God made us in His image with the ability t choose...even wrong things. God warns us not to even touc this tree for He requires us to show our love through our re liance on, and obedience to, Him. God's wisdom is for thos who love him to obey Him.

We are all creations of God, but we are not all His children. The difference lies in obedience. Adam and Eve were meant to be God's children, but their disobedience turned them into creations. Today, we have a chance to choose, to return to being His children, to go back to "The Tree." Our original purpose is to be His children, to draw close to Him, to serve Him as Jesus did, and spread His love. It's about making the connection with God and serving God again as his children. We are his offspring, and just like seeds in this world, we are to reach out to others and help them choose life. This is what God has purposed for us; to be an influence and make a difference.

Wrap-up: By igniting passion for Christ and offering the tree of everlasting life, God takes the initiative to deepen our devotion and offer eternal significance, inviting us into intimate communion with Him.

Reflective Questions:

How do you cultivate passion for Christ and maintain spiritual fervor in your relationship with Him?

Reflect on the concept of everlasting life and its implications for your faith journey. How does the promise of eternity with God influence your perspective on life?

15

The Words That Curse, The Words that Bless

Look at Deuteronomy 27:9-26. By Moses, with the priests' instructions, the people of the tribe of Levi must speak curses in loud voices and the people must agree with the curses by saying "Amen!" It may sound crazy, but this is how curses work. Anyone can put a curse on a person by just saying it! Sounds a bit wild, huh? But here's the scoop: words are super powerful, especially when they're not nice. Think about it – if someone calls you names or bullies you, it messes with your confidence, right? How many of us have experienced being called something when we were young, or at any point in our lives for that matter, and we still have to overcome that inner voice that says it's the truth about us. It's as if the words stick to us like superglue.

It works the opposite way too. Once I was a permanent

substitute teacher for a kindergarten class in Brazil, and there was this child who was struggling. Turns out, his mom thought he'd struggle too, simply because his brother did. I encouraged her not to draw comparisons between the two boys. I thought long and hard about what I could do to have influence in this boy's life. Because I know what the Bible says about blessings and curses and their relationship to what we speak. I told the child he was smart and could learn fast. I also told him he was not destined to be his brother. Long story short, he blossomed and began to learn faster, speak better, and write better. Words really do matter!

Now, in Deuteronomy 28, it says that blessings, not curses, are in store. We can use words to say good things over our lives and the lives of our family and over every aspect of life – it's a game-changer. It's about doing what God says and living life to the fullest. You can't go around cursing people and expect good things to happen – that's just not how it works. I make it a habit to speak good things over my children. I always called my sons good, blessed, smart, strong, prosperous and handsome. I am careful to always speak positive words over them. I know that words have power, and some words stick, good or bad! Look closer at Deuteronomy 28; it's God's promise list!

> Now it shall come to pass, if you diligently obey the voice of the LORD your God, to observe carefully all His commandments which I command you today, that the LORD your God will set you high above all nations of the earth. And all these blessings shall come upon you and overtake you, because you obey the voice of the LORD your God: "Blessed shall you be in the city,

and blessed shall you be in the country. "Blessed shall be the fruit of your body, the produce of your ground and the increase of your herds, the increase of your cattle and the offspring of your flocks. "Blessed shall be your basket and your kneading bowl. "Blessed shall you be when you come in, and blessed shall you be when you go out. "The LORD will cause your enemies who rise against you to be defeated before your face; they shall come out against you one way and flee before you seven ways. "The LORD will command the blessing on you in your storehouses and in all to which you set your hand, and He will bless you in the land which the LORD your God is giving you. "The LORD will establish you as a holy people to Himself, just as He has sworn to you, if you keep the commandments of the LORD your God and walk in His ways. Then all peoples of the earth shall see that you are called by the name of the LORD, and they shall be afraid of you. And the LORD will grant you plenty of goods, in the fruit of your body, in the increase of your livestock, and in the produce of your ground, in the land of which the LORD swore to your fathers to give you. The LORD will open to you His good treasure, the heavens, to give the rain to your land in its season, and to bless all the work of your hand. You shall lend to many nations, but you shall not borrow. And the LORD will make you the head and not the tail; you shall be above only, and not be beneath, if you heed the commandments of the LORD your God, which I command you today, and are careful to observe them. So, you shall not turn aside from any of the words which I command you this day, to the right or the left, to go after other gods to serve them. (Deuteronomy 28:1-14 NKJV)

That's why obeying the Lord is very important. Blessing will come, and curses will be broken! Here is a sample of prayer that one might pray to break curses.

"Lord, please help me to follow your instructions, make me a blessing in your eyes. Never let me utter any curses over anyone else's life and break any curses that have come through other words spoken over my life. In the name of Jesus, by your authority, I'm breaking any curses on me and my family. Lord, I command that every curse be broken in Jesus' name. Amen!"

The Gap

We all have an empty place in us. I have always said to my friends that there is an empty spot in each one of us that only God can fill. This empty spot has been in each one of us since Adam and Eve's initial sin was committed. We all tend to look for something or someone to fill the emptiness that only God can fill with his God given purpose. We tend to try to fill the gaps with what the world says we need, finding out that these things are shallow and unfulfilling. Pursuits like surface pleasures, money, prideful pursuits, worldly recognition. These things are temporary and do not fulfill us. Some of us look for it in what we consume; rich food, alcohol and even drugs. They are all temporary. Nothing can take the place of Jesus in our lives. Trying to fill this gap with anything but Jesus is like asking a gasoline engine to run on diesel. It looks like fuel, but it won't work and will cause damage to the engine. Your engine may run for a minute, but it will break down t is the same thing when we try to fill our heart with lies of the enemy (earthly things). Spiritually we cannot function like God intended for us to. God wants us to be successful and complete.

The Bible says in Galatians 5:19-23 (NKJV), "*Now the works of the flesh are evident, which are: adultery, fornication, uncleanness, lewdness, idolatry, sorcery, hatred, contentions, jealousies, outbursts of wrath, selfish ambitions, dissensions, heresies, envy, murders, drunkenness, revelries, and the like; of which I tell you beforehand, just as I also told you in time past, that those who practice such things will not inherit the kingdom of God. But the fruit of the Spirit is love, joy, peace, longsuffering, kindness, goodness, faithfulness, gentleness, self-control. Against such there is no law.*"

For a few years, I tried to fill the "gap" in my life, seeking happiness in worldly pursuits and choosing paths that went against God's will. Unfortunately, the consequences were real—I experienced paranoia, mental illness, disease, and overall unhappiness. It's important to note that God grants us the freedom to choose, but our choices may not always lead to what's genuinely good for us. Sometimes, they serve as lessons that shape our understanding. This time of my life served as a profound learning experience, akin to going back to school. God uses everything. Everyday challenges and experiences taught me valuable lessons about God. Life itself became a school of wisdom, challenging me to choose to open my heart to what God had for me, or to choose the opposite, to harden it—a decision only I could make. Interestingly, we are all given this choice. My choice was to open my heart and allow God to work in my life and my "gap" began to be filled with true joy, replacing all of the misery caused from past ungodly decisions.

One might think that if we distance ourselves from God He is no longer near us. However, that's not the case with God. God is like the light switch in your house, always there full of power just waiting to be engaged by you. God reassures us, saying, "Don't be afraid, I'm with you; don't tremble with fear, I'm your God" (Isaiah 41:10). This highlights the comforting presence of God, even in moments when we might feel separated from Him.

Wrap-up: Through the power of words and blessings and filling the gap with God's purpose, God initiates transformative communication and purposeful living, inviting us to speak life and fulfill His plans.

Reflective Questions:

How do you use the power of your words aligned with Gods word to bless others and speak life into challenging situations?

Reflect on a time when you discovered God's purpose for your life and filled a gap with His guidance to seek it out. How did it impact your sense of fulfillment and direction?

16

False Teachings

In today's world, there's a growing acceptance of a false notion that all religions lead to the one true God. However, when we closely examine the teachings of Jesus in the Bible, we find that while He advocated for peace and love, this did not mean that He was advocating for us to accept anything outside of the truth of God. Keeping the peace and loving does not mean agreement with a false belief. He was also against false beliefs, and He boldly declared it in scripture.

"I am the way and the truth and the life. No one comes to the Father except through me." (John 14:6 NKJV)

Since the beginning of the time, humanity has faced the struggle of believing in the one true God versus false gods. This can be a challenge for those of us who were raised from

ildren acknowledging false gods. I have personally experi-
nced the shift from believing in false gods, having explored
different religions. I can firmly tell you from personal experience that after experiencing the one true living God that
resonate with the scripture Isaiah 44:7-8 which states that
here is no god besides the Lord.

Churches are sacrificing the harder truth for the soft
acceptance of a lie. In order to seem friendly and welcom-
ng, churches are no longer challenging false beliefs; they are
no longer standing up for the truth. Leaning on their own
worldly wisdom instead of the truth of God. Churches are
increasingly prioritizing what is popular over what is true in
the eyes of God, according to His Word. The road to hell is
wide and the appeal of a carnal, sinful lifestyle may please
people, but contradicts God. Following His commandments
requires turning away from sin. We must acknowledge that
our actions, what we choose to stand for, reflect our hearts.
Though our journey to pursue God is often imperfect, embracing God's guidance moves us closer to His perfect will in
our lives. When we are walking in Gods will, we benefit from
the blessings and protection that being in His will provides.

When I invited Jesus into my heart, transformative changes
began to unfold in my life. He is the truth and is living water.
We will never thirst again when we are in Him. In pressing
into the truth of God, He has revealed the vast possibilities
for my life, and He will reveal yours, too; those that are only
available through Him. Because of this, my false beliefs crum-
bled. The process took time for me, and to this day I continue
to grow in knowledge and truth as Christ continues to work
within me.

If you are entangled in false beliefs, I recommend th
prayer.

Prayer for Deliverance from False Beliefs

"Lord, Jesus, help me see the way you see. Help me to see; to
see your truth and no other. Open my eyes and heart to your
living waters, where your Holy Spirit can touch and cleanse my
soul. Break any ungodly contracts with evil in my life. Cover
me with your Holy Hands and deliver me from the evil one.
Remove the veil of evil from my eyes, Lord, Jesus, and allow me
to receive your salvation. Open the door to Heavenly Wisdom.
Guide me to live closer to you, for your presence alone fills me.
Thank you, Lord. Amen!"

Prepare for God's Revolution

What is a spiritual revolution? A spiritual revolution refers t
a profound and transformative shift in spiritual beliefs, prac
tices, and consciousness within individuals or communitie
Unlike political or social revolutions that focus on change
in governance or societal structures, a spiritual revolutio
entails a fundamental reorientation of one's inner life, value
and worldview.

It is time for us to open ourselves to the mighty wor
of God, allowing His power and fire to operate at their ful
potential. As we dedicate our time to God, He starts workin
in us, preparing us for greatness and filling us with His powe
to be used at full capacity. As he began the transformativ
work in me, He urged me to engage more in His work

Despite feeling unprepared, I realized, all I need to do is allow Him to work wonders through me.

Within my circle of friends, united in our love for serving God, our meetings become a space where God's power is unleashed. The Holy Spirit manifests in a powerful way, revealing His holy fire, breaking bondages, and dispelling curses. When we gather for meetings, God is present, ready to perform miracles, signs, and wonders.

I encourage you to do the same – permit the Holy Spirit to manifest His power in your life. Let God manifest his power in you, through the gifts of the Holy Spirit, speaking in tongues, revelation of the word, prophecies, and healing. Don't limit Him to one thing. They can all manifest at the same time allowing God to do what he does best, use us as willing vessels of His supernatural holy fire to change the world! You don't need to be perfect or qualified; Jesus died for us while we were still sinners. None of us will ever be flawless, but through His work on the cross, Jesus took away our sins and paid our debts. In order to engage in His work, simply ask Him, "God, please use me today for Your kingdom to be manifested on Earth. Let Your kingdom come, and Your will be done on Earth as it is in Heaven!"

It's time for us to allow God's mighty work to be used to its full potential. When we open our time to God, He will begin to work on us and use us at full capacity. We will be filled with faith and expectation ready to be used. I can testify to the works he has begun in me. Every day I grow, and He encourages me to do more on His behalf.

Sometimes I am not ready for all that He has for me to do. Then I realize that all I have to do is lean in and He lovingly prepares me for the work He has for me. I encourage you to make godly friends and get around people who love and serve the Lord. Worship together, read the Bible, study it together and God will show up. He will begin to break bondages, heal the sick, and manifest His miracles in your life.

Wrap-up: By discerning false teachings and preparing for God's revolution in your life, God initiates a process of spiritual discernment and readiness, equipping us to stand firm in truth and righteousness.

Reflective Questions:

How do you discern false teachings and remain steadfast in your faith amidst cultural and doctrinal shifts?

Reflect on a time when you felt called to take a stand for truth or righteousness. What challenges did you face, and how did you respond?

17

All Things Work Together for Good with the Lord

In this chapter, I invite you into a tapestry of interconnected stories—little truths I've encountered through daily moments and quiet reflections guided by the Holy Spirit. Each vignette carries its own significance, woven together by the common thread of divine revelation and spiritual insight. Through these glimpses into my life, I hope to illuminate the profound wisdom that lies within the seemingly mundane, reminding us that every moment holds the potential for spiritual growth and revelation when viewed through the lens of faith.

We Are the Bride of Christ

We are the bride of Christ, spiritually. We are supposed to have closeness with the Lord. When God seeks our time, it's an invitation to intimacy. Intimacy with God is spending personal time with Him and giving Him your undivided attention. Some people have prayer closets where they get away with the Lord. I never could find a place in my house like a small closet or a special room that separated me from everywhere else and allowed me to just focus on Jesus. It's weird I am saying that, but it's true! Sometimes I admit I have a tough time reading my Bible and praying. I know other Christians struggle with the same thing. Life has so many distractions for so many of us. I have found that finding a dedicated space for prayer or Bible reading has been a challenge, but I've discovered that listening to worship songs serves as a meaningful way for me to channel my attention to the Lord. Finding a good Christian radio station has been a key for me. Whether driving, resting, or writing, I've made praising Him a natural habit, creating a mindset of adoration and praise.

Intimacy with Jesus parallels the depth of connection in a marriage, where increased intimacy leads to better communication and a better life. I feel his presence, and I believe my worship of Him is like a sweet fragrance to Him! My intimacy with Jesus is growing more every day. I praise Him everywhere. If I'm driving, He is driving with me. If I am resting, He is resting with me. If I am writing, He is writing with me. I have found there is no place where I can't praise Him. I have created the habit of adoration, and sometimes I am in a conversation with Him constantly. The more time spend with God, the more it comes naturally without any pressure or imposition. I just do it. In Psalms it says I can't escape from His presence.

> Where can I go from your Spirit?
> Where can I flee from your presence?
> If I go up to the heavens, you are there.
> if I make my bed in the depths, you are there.
> (Psalm 139:7-8 NIV)

Just as a lack of intimacy can strain marital relationships, losing intimacy with Jesus leaves us empty and distanced from the awareness of His love, resulting in confusion and misery. Only in His presence can we realize our full potential. We are truly empowered by His incredible love and grace. Your time with the Lord is uniquely special. Without His love, we are nothing more than dust in a desert. Let God be your everything and create a habit of praise so that you can bloom in His presence.

Retreating Yourself

In the midst of my first guest speaking engagement at a Christian women's retreat, I anticipated teaching a specific topic. However, God had other plans. Instead of following my prepared notes, I decided to submit to the Holy Spirit during my time with the leaders and in prayer.

As I entered the stunning retreat location in Galveston, Texas, organized by a wonderful group led by Pastor Brenda and Mary Moreno, I sensed God's presence. The house was beautiful, filled with a diverse group of women ranging from their 30s to 70s. The atmosphere was charged with anticipation. During my preparations in the room, Miss Brenda, one of the leaders, sat with me and began to pray. Her godly word brought a calmness and focus that I desperately needed. I felt assured the Holy Spirit was with me, guiding my words.

Although I had prayed and asked God what to say, I was not sure of what I would say. When I was in a quiet place with the Lord, He revealed the word "Brand." Uncertain about its meaning, I sought His guidance. In conversations with the women, particularly one who shared her life story of being controlled by her husband, I realized the profound significance of societal branding and the need for freedom.

This experience taught me a powerful lesson: when we prioritize the Holy Spirit's plans over our own plans, God orchestrates wonderful experiences, unveiling insights beyond our expectations. The retreat became a transformative moment, affirming the importance of letting go and allowing God to lead me, trusting His revelations. So, when I spoke that night, I put away my notes and went with what God was speaking. For the women who felt branded, it was a transformative experience transcending into a new identity of who Christ says we are versus who the world says we are. We were cleansed by the fire of the Holy Spirit that night. It was truly a powerful night of Gods joy!

Opening Everything to the Lord

As I opened one of Max Lucado's books, a profound message struck me: "Open every pore of your soul to God" presence." Being a cosmetologist and a medical aesthetician, I understand pores as the small openings on our skin's surface. Scientifically, they allow microscopic particles to pass. Impurities often accumulate through these pores, leading to various skin issues. The solution? A good facial, deep cleansing, and proper skincare for radiant refreshment! Similarly, our souls have pores that absorb every particle of God's light. However, we need to allow it in. God doesn't force His way. Our souls must cry out, saying, "Fill me, Lord!" If our soul's pores carry impurities like negativity, anger, envy, addiction, evil thoughts, obsessions, unhappiness, or fear, Jesus will come and cleanse them. He purifies our soul, casting out its enemies, and leaves us with a renewed, born-again soul where His light never fades.

When we open every pore of our soul to Him, He initiates a cleansing process, removing the enemies of our soul, casting them out and creating a brand new you. Jesus continues this work until the end of times, granting our soul a new beginning; infinite opportunities on Earth and in Heaven. How can we experience this soul cleansing by Jesus? "*Ask, and it will be given to you; seek, and you will find; knock, and the door will be opened to you,*" says Matthew 7:7 (NKJV). Asking God is essential for all our answers. You can ask for the cleansing of your soul. When you ask Jesus to be your savior and become His follower, He not only cleanses your soul but also changes and challenges you forever, with all other essential things added.

God Wastes Nothing

We never know what God will use to teach us. Everything we see and touch God uses. He wastes nothing. He can use every moment of our lives to teach us his vast truths and to interconnect us with our Christian family to strengthen and encourage us in our walk. It is God's desire to let us know that we are never alone, and He is with us in all things. The following memoirs reflect how God has been with me in my walk, even in the smallest happenings in my life.

The Candlelight Holder

Remember you are God's masterpiece! I gazed at the candle holder, adorned with an exquisite antique painting, resting on my dining table. The fusion of colors creating its unique appearance fascinated me. The painter intentionally crafted layers of colors to achieve a vintage look, mirroring life's complexities. As I observed, God spoke to me, unveiling the symbolism: "Can you see these layers? They represent the pains, sorrows, and life's experiences that shaped you. Just like the layers on this holder, your character has been formed through the scratches of life. The pains made you who you are, and your uniqueness shines through, just like this candle holder. I am the painter, and you are the masterpiece. I am designing and transforming you, taking care of what is mine. From the womb, I formed you, knowing every detail - your character, personality, and talents - all hand-painted by Me," declared the Lord.

Reflecting on God's revelation, it resonated with the

transformative process. In my own artistic endeavors, especially chalk painting on furniture, I understood the beauty of layering. Applying base colors, layering, scratching, and sanding creates an antique effect. The final result, initially seemingly ugly, transforms into something fabulous with each layer. It dawned on me – just as aging enhances our beauty, the experiences in life shape us. God, the master artist, intricately details our lives with His powerful hands. We are His unique masterpieces, hand crafted by the ultimate Creator. Our individuality highlights His amazing artistry. We are His "Obra Prima," a testament to His perfection.

Observing the world around me, I see the strokes of His ongoing masterpiece, a reminder that only God, the true Author, can breathe life into His creations. God uses everything in life to teach and develop us into beautiful masterpieces.

A Lifeless Bluebird

One day, as I left work, I noticed a lifeless blue bird by the door, adorned with beautiful feathers. Compassion filled me for this small creature, which was lying dead on the ground. At that moment, I felt God speaking to me: "See this dead blue bird? It was full of life that I gave, but the wind came, knocked it out of its tree, and it died. Do you know what this means?" As I reflected on the question, God taught me a valuable lesson. Despite appearances, we must find beauty in everything. Even in moments that seem bad or unpleasant.

Jesus emphasized the deeper truth – that though it may be dead to us here, there is still life, eternal life. Because of Christ, we have hope. The bird may pass away, but in Christ the bird has eternity. Jesus said the world will pass away, but my words and promises to my people will endure.

When death is close, our instinct is to run away in fear. Yet, with Jesus, nothing is impossible with His living water of life. He reminded me of His sacrifice on the cross. It was not for Himself, but for us and our families. His death had a greater purpose – to save many souls and bring them back to the Father, the Creator, the Alpha and Omega.

Even as Christians we die, and our spirits no longer exist in our bodies. However, we have the promise to endure with Christ. Jesus reassured me that this bird soars with all of His creation in eternity. There is also another kind of death where people seem spiritually dead when distant from Jesus, much like the blue bird cast from its tree, losing protection and falling to the ground. Yet, Jesus reassured me that there is always hope for them to soar!

Broken Vase

In one of the many instances the Lord used to teach me, I had a vision. The Lord revealed a shattered vase. I marveled at the broken pieces; and He revealed to me a profound truth – God overlooks our brokenness and envisions us as mended by His boundless love. In His eyes, through Him, we are not fractured, but instead we are like perfectly crafted vases, hand shaped by His divine artistry. Despite any former brokenness, through Christ, God sees us as flawless in His divine presence, untouched by imperfections. Satan, our adversary, may emphasize our brokenness in an attempt to sow confusion about who we are as God's creation. Yet, we can be assured

at in God's divine presence, we stand whole and unblem-
hed. If you ever to feel like a shattered vase, remember this:
Jesus' eyes, you are a beautiful, perfect vessel. Now, fill your
fe with the living water of His presence.

he Doll Makeover

ne day as an adult I was having trouble sleeping. You know
nose nights when you toss and turn, and your brain will not
nut off. Bottom line, I was frustrated with my inability to
eep. So, I began to pray and ask the Lord for help to rest in
is presence. I was laying there with my eyes closed, and I saw
ttle white doves before my eyes like the ones you see inside
sand dollar at the beach when it's broken open. This was a
gn to me that God was revealing something to me.

A distant memory began to flash in front of my eyes of
hen I was a child, and it was Christmas. Our family was
aving financial problems, and that year my family could not
fford to buy Christmas gifts. My mother was a seamstress, so
ne decided to redress one of my dolls and give it a makeover.
n spite of her new clothes, I recognized the doll as the same
ne. I was so disappointed because I knew it was my own doll!
knew that how I reacted hurt my mother. So, the lesson here
life may deal us disappointments, but it is how we respond
o them that matters. Once again in my life, as an adult,
was Christmas, and money was tight. I had spent days in
y bed crying and disappointed over my financial troubles.
on't get me wrong, I know God will meet my needs, but
this point I was having a straight-out pity party, just like
hen I was five years old. God was giving the same advice he

must have given my parents when my mother faced her do
challenge. God was saying, "Quit having a pity party and ge
creative!" Ah! This challenge was only a challenge if I qu
believing God for a creative answer. I began to pray, receive
peace, and got busy. Every need was met that Christmas. N
more sleepless nights. No more letting the devil play with m
mind. I knew God had me, and He always provides a way.

My Loaves and Fishes Moment

Remember the story with Jesus and the loaves and fishe
Jesus was teaching a multitude of people. He noticed tha
it was getting late, and the people were getting hungry. Th
disciples said to send the people away so they may have tim
to go home and get food, but Jesus said to them, "You fee
them." The disciples were confused and said it would tak
eight months' wages to feed them! However, Jesus challenge
them, saying, "You give them something to eat." Despite thei
doubts, Jesus miraculously multiplied five loaves and tw
fishes, satisfying everyone. I know that it is possible for Go
to manifest anything we need in order to fulfill his purpos
We must simply take what we have, bless it, and give i
to Him.

One day I ordered food, just enough for myself. A youn
man delivered it. The Holy Spirit prompted me to invit
him to share the meal, and he agreed. Although the foo
only appeared to be enough for one person, every bite multi
plied, leaving both of us full. During our conversation, H
shared that he was currently distant from God and partici
pated in secular comedy shows at night. Prompted by God

encouraged him to return to Christian comedy. Despite the limited food, each bite multiplied, and our plates were never empty. We continued eating until he exclaimed, "I'm so full!" He left, still with food on his plate and mine. Jesus was in the midst of us, and the young man was amazed by the miraculous multiplication. I expressed my desire to see him perform Christian comedy, and he agreed, thanking me, and acknowledging my kindness. He said no one whom he delivered food to had ever offered to have lunch together. He called me a very good person, which was a blessing to me and unbeknownst to him made my day.

This moment, orchestrated by Jesus, not only provided a divine word to the young man but produced a miracle for us to witness and created a newfound friendship. Through this divine intervention, I discovered he was a Christian comedian who had strayed from his faith. God used this meal and my obedience to share what I had to encourage him to return to Christian comedy. The young man left astonished by God's love for him and God's divine intervention. I was blessed not only with a delicious meal, but a new friend. Through this shared meal, God's grace multiplied, allowing for a deep and meaningful conversation about spiritual renewal and trans-formation. Just as Jesus blessed the multitude with abun-dance, so too does He provide for our needs and orchestrates moments of connection and renewal in unexpected ways.

Holding on Tight to Miracles

The more I serve the Lord, the more I witness His hands at work in people's lives. It constantly teaches me new lessons about holding on to the truth of God and keeping the miracles he gives. As a prayer partner in my local church, I actively pray and serve, finding joy in it. One day, the pastor called us to pray for people, and as they gathered at the altar, I prayed before joining them. On this particular day, I sensed something special was going to happen. A lady I hadn't seen before approached me, seeking prayer for her immobile finger. I spoke what Jesus guided me to say, asking if she believed in Jesus as the great physician. She affirmed, and the Holy Spirit touched her and her finger was healed. However, when she returned to her seat, her finger worsened. Distressed, she approached me, asking about the deterioration. I encouraged her not to let the devil steal her healing, declaring that Jesus had performed a surgery on her finger. I rebuked the lies of the enemy, touched her finger, and, by the authority God gave me, declared her finger released in Jesus' name. I spoke to her what Jesus told me to say. Keep your blessing do not let the enemy steal what God has done for you, by convincing you that it did not happen. Remember what I said about words, they matter. Fellow Christians, do not curse yourself by saying what the enemy wants you to say about you. Keep God's words of healing close to you and do not let them go.

God's My Attorney

Remember, no matter what the circumstance, you can call on God. One day God was my Attorney. At one time in my life, I was confronted with a legal issue. I worried for months that I would be going to court without any legal representation. I prayed, and in a dream, God showed me an arch with an eagle on it. I did not know what it meant. On the way to court, I had a revelation moment when a white bird which reminded me of a dove almost collided with the windshield. I sensed that I was to see it as a sign that God was in the midst, and at that moment, the undeniable presence of the Holy Spirit was there, assuring me that God's divine guidance would be inside the courtroom. As we entered the courtroom, I looked up and saw a massive wooden arch and an eagle, precisely as had been revealed in the dream months earlier. I knew from this confirmation that God was there to advocate for me. He would be there with me, like he was with Daniel in the lion's den. It does not matter what kind of situation you are in. God is there with you. Trust in the Lord with all of your heart and know that he is there for you.

Wrap-up: Through embracing intimacy with God and recognizing divine lessons in everyday moments, God initiates a journey of intimacy and revelation, inviting us to seek His presence and wisdom in all things.

Reflective Questions:

How do you cultivate intimacy with God and prioritize time with Him in your daily life?

Reflect on a recent experience where you encountered a divine lesson in an unexpected moment. What did you learn about God's character and His desire to communicate with you?

18

Who Is God?

This chapter deals with some of the basic questions we are asked as Christians about who God is and why things are the way they are. Not every question you will ever ask will be answered, but I believe in God's divine direction for you for those questions to be answered.

God is Simple

Have you ever tried to explain God? I often think that God can be both simple and complex simultaneously. Have you ever noticed some of the weird ways He directed Moses to lead God's people from slavery to the promised land? His methods at times may seem unconventional – like instructing Moses to break a rock for water or to part a sea wide enough to swallow an army!

The stories of these miracles are just a glimpse of His

character. God revealed to the prophets the coming of Jesus right down to the smallest detail. Today, God continues to perform miracles, using people of all ages and backgrounds to fulfill His purpose on Earth. Despite the changing times, His words remain true and eternal.

How do we know true prophets from false ones? While I could share more examples of how God works through people, it's essential to discern false prophets. So how do you know what the truth is, and what is the lie when it comes to prophets. First and foremost, you must study the word of God and know what God says about a matter. Their actions and teachings should align with the Bible. You must take time to read and understand biblical principles to distinguish between God's true revelations versus man's personal inspirations.

Complicated yet simple, yes! God is wonderful and loving, who covers those who believe in Him. He reveals Himself to those who follow Him. He gives direction to his children who seek to obey His will.

Stumbling Blocks

We must ask God to help us in steering clear of the allure of materialism and its distractions. The Son of man, Jesus, is as simple as He is complex. We have to peel back many layers to understand the depth of what Christ has done for us. Our sin debt being paid is simple, why He did it for us is deep and is the definition of God's deep profound love for us. God is love forever deep and many faceted; simple, yet complicated.

Jesus embodies this magnificent love, revealed through His

Spirit. This love disarms spiritual bondages, breaking chains and elevating us to a level of purity and dignity, reconnecting us with our Father God and His abundance. Despite our sins, God does not abandon us to the hands of our enemy Satan or his spirits of vengeance, jealousy, covetousness, fornication, gossip, murder, or any other dark spirits. He remains simple in His truth: calling upon the name of Jesus assures salvation as stated in the following scriptures.

> And everyone who calls on the name of the Lord will be saved;...
> (Joel 2:32 and Acts 2:21 NIV)

> For 'whoever calls on the name of the Lord shall be saved.'
> (Romans 10:13 NKJV)

Living for Jesus

Many believers think God is someone far off in Heaven who doesn't really care about what happens to them here on Earth. They question why God would allow certain things to happen to them. As humans created by God, living for God is our goal, and we are to live our lives based on His truth and follow His commandments. There is nothing in the Bible that says we will not face trials or hardships. The disciples who lived with Jesus, and lived after Jesus, faced many troubles. The early followers of Jesus and His friends dealt with suffering and persecution even unto death. Despite knowing Jesus well, they went through difficult times. [Source: https://bible.knowing-jesus.com/topics/Christ-s-Disciples-Will-Suffer]

When we suffer, we can't blame others. Bad things happen

to good people, and there's a saying about it being both right and wrong. I remember my aunt blaming her mother for all the bad things in her life. However, blaming others only exacerbates the problem. It's easier to blame than to accept our own faults. The blame game needs to stop, but people sometimes blame others because facing their problems is too painful. As I've lived, I've realized the complexity of our emotions. It's easy to live in the flesh, but it's hard to let the Holy Spirit lead and let go of things we hold on to for various reasons.

Living for Jesus was a challenging decision for His disciples. Jesus told them to leave everything behind and follow Him, a command that extends to all generations. It wasn't just leaving family and friends, but about letting go of everything that enslaves us. Bad things happen to everyone, and we can't control everything. In those moments, Jesus tells us to let Him take care of our burdens, not to look back, and to trust Him to handle the situation. Let it GO!

The Blame Game: Is it Eve's fault?

The story of Adam and Eve in paradise often draws blame towards Eve for succumbing to the serpent's lies, with many attributing our current sin situation to her actions. Let's take a moment to ponder this and discover truth.

Picture paradise where God's blessings for humanity begins with Adam and Eve. It's a place of incredible beauty, abundant with flowers, animals, and every imaginable creation. God, the Creator, crafted this haven to delight mankind. Imagine for yourself, the unmatched harmony of birds singing, flowers blooming, and delicious mouthwatering fruit all around. Everything is easily accessible, and all creatures coexist peacefully.

Now, Satan enters the scene in the form of a talking snake. He begins to tempt Eve to disobey God, suggesting that eating the fruit that God had forbidden will grant her knowledge and power and implying that she would be like God. The blame game might have started in paradise, but it came from hell. Satan had been waiting for an opportunity to cast guilt and condemnation upon the woman created to help God and man.

The blame game kicks into full gear when Eve, convinced by the snake's words, takes a bite of the forbidden fruit, and then offers it to Adam. Adam then believes the lie and eats the fruit. Then, when confronted by God, Adam places the blame on Eve. How often do we, like Adam, shift responsibility for our actions by saying, "My friend told me to do it?"

Reflecting on personal experiences, I recall my teenage years when friends offered me drugs. Despite the temptation, I said "NO" because my parents shared stories of a family member's struggles with addiction. Adam, too, could have resisted, but he succumbed, forgetting God's guidance. When God questions Adam and Eve about their whereabouts, it's not because He doesn't know. It's about highlighting the broken trust in their relationship. The blame game continues as they hide and feel shame.

This echoes our daily struggles, breaking commandments, believing worldly lies, and often blaming others for our choices.

In the midst of our struggles, it becomes crucial to accept Jesus into our lives. Allowing the Holy Spirit to fortify us with God's words, we find freedom. Only through forgiveness and understanding God's power within us can we break free from the condemnation of Adam and Eve and overcome the blame game as men and women of God.

This happens with us every day. We break the commandments, we sin and do exactly the same, believing the world's lies and letting them control us. We are snared by our belief in the lie. We are also snared by not taking responsibility for the sin in the first place and by blaming someone else for the decisions we make to sin. The world offers us every excuse to act against God. It is quick to offer an excuse by saying it was anyone's fault but our own.

When we are in the flesh, our spirit is in bondage and is screaming for the freedom that only God can give us. That is why it is important to accept Jesus as our personal savior, and to make him Lord of our life. We need to let God fortify us through Jesus, the Holy Spirit and by God's word. Christ alone can set us free from the blame game. He can free us from condemnation we saw in The Garden of Eden.

Citizen of Heaven

Did you know that you become a citizen of Heaven when you accept Jesus Christ as your personal savior and repent of your sins? The Lord's Prayer has always intrigued me. It's a profound prayer that I've meditated on and explored through various explanations. Jesus taught His disciples how to pray. It's recorded in Matthew 6:9-13 and Luke 11:2-4. Commonly known as The Lord's Prayer, it goes like this:

Our Father, which art in heaven,
Hallowed be thy name.
Thy kingdom come,
Thy will be done in earth, as it is in heaven.
Give us this day our daily bread,
and forgive us our debts,
As we forgive our debtors.
And lead us not into temptation,
but deliver us from evil.
For thine is the kingdom, and the power, and the glory forever.
Amen.

While recited in church services and personal prayers, the essence of this prayer is crucial. Jesus imparted its importance, emphasizing it as a prayer for the Kingdom – a dominion governed by rules and laws. The Kingdom of God, mentioned by Jesus throughout the New Testament, is portrayed as a spiritual reality rather than a physical place. In Mark 1:14-15, Jesus announces its nearness, urging repentance and belief in the gospel (good news) for entry.

When I applied for U.S. citizenship, I had to follow rules, submit documents, pay fees, and undergo an interview to assess my suitability within the country's laws. Similarly, Jesus' teachings about the Kingdom of God stirred controversy among religious leaders as they grappled with the concept. This Kingdom, not a physical realm but a spiritual reality, reflects God's rule and reign over all creation. It is open to those with childlike faith, characterized by love, justice, and peace.

Accepting citizenship in His Kingdom involves repentance

(turning away from) from sin and acknowledging Jesus a your Savior. This step aligns with Jesus' teachings, challengin us to contribute to a more just and compassionate worl The Kingdom of God, an integral aspect of Jesus' messag continues to inspire Christians to live out its principles i our daily lives.

Wrap-up: By understanding God and His kingdom an embracing citizenship in Heaven, God initiates a perspectiv shift and eternal perspective, inviting us to align our live with His eternal purposes and promises.

Reflective Questions:

How does your understanding of God's kingdom influence the wa you live and make decisions in the present?

Reflect on the concept of citizenship in heaven and its implication for your identity and priorities. How does knowing your eterna destination impact the way you live on earth?

19

⚜

Embracing New Beginnings

As we come to the close of this journey together, I want to offer you an invitation—an invitation to embrace new beginnings in your life through a personal relationship with Jesus Christ. Whether you're already walking with God or just beginning to explore faith, there is always room for growth, renewal, and deeper intimacy with our Creator. If you desire to accept Jesus as your Lord and Savior or recommit your life to Him, I invite you to pray this simple prayer with me:

"Lord Jesus, I come to you today, acknowledging that I am a sinner in need of your forgiveness. I believe that you died on the cross for my sins and rose again from the dead. I repent of my sins and ask for your forgiveness. Please come into my heart, be

my Lord and Savior, and guide me in the paths of righteousness.
Thank you for your love and grace. In Jesus' name, amen."

If you prayed this prayer sincerely, congratulations! You have taken the first step towards a new life in Christ. Now, I encourage you to take the following steps:

1. Find a Bible-based Church

Seek out a local church where you can connect with other believers, grow in your faith, and receive spiritual support and guidance. Look for a church that teaches the Bible as the inspired Word of God and emphasizes the importance of a personal relationship with Jesus Christ. Jesus said in His word He would send the Holy Spirit to help us in our walk with Christ and to defeat the enemy of this world, Satan. A Bible-based church is one that recognizes the power and the presence of the Holy Spirit in our lives and in the world today. He is the Spirit of God, ever present, with love, grace, wisdom and power and there to lead us in all things. The ideal church should acknowledge the profound influence of the Holy Spirit, embracing His guidance, healing, miraculous interventions, and the spiritual gifts promised to believers. Begin your search by inviting the Holy Spirit to direct you towards a congregation where you can nurture your faith and discover God's purpose for your life.

2. Develop a Personal Relationship with God

Set aside time each day to study the Bible, pray, meditate on God's Word, worship, and exercise your faith. Cultivate intimacy with God through regular communication and communion with Him.

3. Share Your Faith

As you grow in your relationship with God, share the good news of salvation with others. Your testimony and witness can be a powerful tool for leading others to Christ and helping them discover God's true purpose for their lives.

4. Walk in Your Purpose

Discover and embrace the unique purpose and gifts that God has given you. Use everything you do—your talents, skills, resources, and opportunities—for the glory of God and the advancement of His kingdom.

Remember, the journey of faith is not always easy, but it is worth it. God promises to be with you every step of the way; guiding, empowering, and transforming you into the person He created you to be. Embrace this new beginning with faith, courage, and expectancy, knowing that God has great plans for your life. Welcome to the family of God!

Wrap-up: After being born-again, and committing to walk in our purpose, remember this journey is one of transformation, growth, and empowerment. As we step into this new chapter of our lives, let us remember that our relationship with God is not static but dynamic, continually growing as we seek Him, trust Him, and walk in obedience to His Word. May we embrace each new day as an opportunity to draw closer to God, fulfill our purpose, and live for His glory.

Reflective Questions:

How has your understanding of God's purpose for your life evolved throughout this journey?

In what ways do you envision yourself using your talents, skills, and resources for the glory of God and the advancement of His kingdom?

s you step into this new beginning, what steps will you take to eepen your relationship with God and walk in alignment with His ill for your life?

you decided for the Lord today, make sure to get a Bible if you o not have one and write the date down in your bible. This is your ansformative moment.

od Bless You!

esiree

About Desiree Dantas

DESIREE DANTAS, originally from Brazil, has called the heart of Texas, USA, home for over twenty years where she is a wife, mother, business owner and public speaker. Desiree's life took a profound turn when she encountered Jesus and heard His voice, setting her on a path illuminated by faith and spiritual revelations. In her captivating book, 'Can I Touch You, Jesus?', Desiree chronicles her myriad of religious experiences, emphasizing the unwavering presence of God throughout her journey.